RAMSBOTTOM'S REVOLUTION

RAMSBOTTOM'S
REVOLUTIONARY DOCTOR

THE LIFE AND TIMES OF PETER MURRAY MCDOUALL

NIGEL JEPSON

YOUCAXTON
PUBLICATIONS

ISBN 978-1-914424-37-3
Published by YouCaxton Publications 2021

YouCaxton Publications
www.youcaxton.co.uk

Front cover: Engraved Portrait of Peter Murray McDouall 1840 - courtesy
of RG Gammage, *History of the Chartist Movement 1837-1853*, (originally
published in 1854 with a second revised edition in 1894) p156.

Contents

ACKNOWLEDGEMENTS

I am grateful to a large number of people, in different ways, for assistance given in carrying out this project.

To start with, I wish to thank Andrew Todd who has been willing throughout to enter into discussion regarding various aspects of the life of Peter Murray McDouall. His expertise, particularly in relation to the seven years in which the Doctor lived in Ramsbottom, has been invaluable to me in researching the topic from the more local standpoint.

Andrew was the inaugural Chairman of Ramsbottom Heritage Society when it was formed in the late 1980s and has written many books and articles on the history and development of the town; whether on McDouall or broader matters, his work is always interestingly compiled and thought-provoking.

As well as providing me with a starting-point, Andrew also helped by lending certain source materials, including a 1918 first edition copy of Mark Hovell's *The Chartist Movement*. Enduring in a fragile, well-thumbed state, I am relieved at this stage to be able to hand it back still just about in one piece!

Thanks also to past RHS contributors, Trevor Park and Alan Hitch, whose articles on McDouall and/or the Grant Brothers have been published in RHS News Magazines; and to the present Chair of the Society, Kate Slingsby, for offering advice relating to other aspects of the town's rich heritage. Brenda Richards has also been helpful in her link role with Bury Library and Archives Centre.

The course of research inevitably led me into contact with different libraries and resource bases. Firstly, my appreciation to all the staff at Ramsbottom Library and Heritage Gallery for providing access to local materials, including exhibition booklets. Next, Bury Library and Archives Centre. In particular, my thanks to Wendy Gradwell who spared no effort in seeking to unearth particular written and pictorial items of interest, particularly from the Carmyllie Collection. Further afield, with regard to McDouall's time spent serving as Ashton-under-Lyne's Chartist delegate, thanks to staff at The Tameside Local Studies & Archive Centre for facilitating access to copies of transcriptions of proceedings from McDouall's two trial hearings as well as many other materials specific to his association with Ashton.

With regard to 'follow-ups' on walks conducted in the Ramsbottom area during lockdown, thanks to Judith Hilton (nee Lees) for agreeing to a viewing of the John Kay plaque on the wall of the privately-owned Park Farm House. Also to John Wilcock of 'John the Jewellers' for allowing me to view the interior of McDouall's one-time medical base situated at 18, Bolton Street. Further indebted to Phil Rose, CEO of Rosebridge Ltd., for taking me on an internal tour of the premises of what had been converted from the Grants Arms but still fascinatingly retaining some of the original features of the building.

I would like to express thanks to Chris Aspin whose stimulating work, with broader focus across the county of Lancashire, proved immensely useful to tap into. I have also greatly appreciated his willingness to enter into discussion on the relevant occasion.

On a similar broader scale within Lancashire, thanks to John Simpson and his work on behalf of the Edenfield History Society, particularly in relation to details regarding the Chatterton Riot of 1826.

∞

At the end of each chapter, headed 'Notes on Sources', acknowledgement has been given to authors of books written about McDouall's life either before he came to work as a doctor in Ramsbottom in 1835 or else covering the time when his horizons expanded after becoming a Chartist leader.

One particular author from this list whose contributions on the subject I would wish to acknowledge is Paul A. Pickering. The work he has carried out on the Chartist period is phenomenally deep and eclectic. Given the focus of this study, bearing directly on the life and times of Peter Murray McDouall, I was grateful to come across two major articles of his, undertaken with respective collaborators S. Roberts and Owen R. Ashton, both providing very instructive insights into the life of McDouall.

The specific articles I am referring to are: *Pills, Pamphlets and Politics* and *The People's Advocate*. Apart from the absorbing content and presentation of each, it was intriguing to latch on to the question posed in both articles as to how and why a full-length biography of McDouall had not been undertaken to date.

'The question' reverberated in my mind and has proved one I obviously felt motivated to address!

I suspect though I have ended up taking on the challenge in a rather different format to that which Paul A. Pickering and his co-writers may have envisaged. However, it was what was alluded to in those articles as 'a gap in the market' that gave added incentive to undertaking this study.

∞

Further, I owe a considerable amount of gratitude to those nearest and dearest for strength and resilience fed through to me to complete the project. Thanks to daughters Sarah and Kathryn for listening to regular 'progress updates'. The author of published works herself, on the theme of linguistics, I was grateful for Sarah's proof-reading skills and other helpful suggestions.

Fundamentally to wife Anna for bearing the brunt of all my battles with technology! Plus her massive support in keeping everything so much alive, on a day-to-day basis, as well as being willing to absorb my wittering on endlessly about this and that aspect of the task in hand.

In short, this book couldn't have been completed without all the above assistance, for which I am immensely grateful.

PREFACE

There are many people, living in present times, who would say that the nature of wealth, power and influence across society is unfairly concentrated in the hands of a privileged minority of the population. If he were alive today, Peter Murray McDouall would most likely be amongst that number.

For certain though, during the period of the first half of the nineteenth century in which McDouall lived, the balance was tipped even more markedly than nowadays in the direction of the favoured few and against the best interests of the vast majority of other people. As well as this, it was highly dangerous for people to point out such discrepancies, let alone publicly protest.

However, McDouall was never one to shrink back from those ideals he cherished and believed in. As a result, he tirelessly championed the cause of the working classes, for example in seeking to bring about improvements in their living and work conditions.

Born in Scotland, he had arrived in Ramsbottom as a 21-year-old starting up a medical practice on Bolton Street. He could have settled for a comfortable life as a doctor but, shocked by the conditions prevalent within the Factory System, he campaigned on behalf of local workers and their families. This was to bring him into opposition with factory-owners such as the Grant Brothers.

∞

This book sets out to show how McDouall's time spent in Ramsbottom from 1835 to 1842 led eventually to him branching out into the Chartist movement and playing a national role as an agitator for reform. In so doing, in the course of arousing the hostility of the authorities, he was to endure extreme hardship, both personally and in relation to the welfare of his family.

It was in Ramsbottom that McDouall first spoke out as a radical voice before events took him further afield on missions he was passionate about fulfilling.

McDouall's journey would bring him into contact, one way and another, with many of the leading political figures of the day. As well as relating the story of the man himself, the book also encapsulates the revealing, broader life and times of Peter Murray McDouall.

∞

As a former history teacher, having once taught a 19th century social and economic course, I confess I never came across reference to McDouall. Quite recently though, I was given the opportunity to put this record straight.

Chapter One will begin with how I happened to come across a particular commemorative tribute to him. More significantly, how the discovery stimulated an ambition to want to tell the extraordinary tale of Peter Murray McDouall's dedication to the cause of achieving wider freedoms and equality for all those people he believed, in one way or another, to be victims of oppression. As such, this story has a resonance extending beyond the immediate period of history in question, raising issues which have continuing relevance up to the present day.

Nigel Jepson, August 31, 2021.

CHAPTER ONE

On the Trail of Dr. McDouall and

the Grant Brothers:

FOUR PLAQUES AND A TOWER

Plaque One: Peter Murray McDouall

Plaques put up on buildings have a natural way of attracting the attention of passers-by. Or so it may be thought. In some instances though, they may prove difficult to pick out in the landscape.

That's my excuse. At least for the fact I'd somehow failed to spot a particular one in the town where I have lived for the past twenty-five years. It's not as if Ramsbottom is a massively big place. Reckoning I must have walked hundreds of times along Bolton Street, I had all the while not noticed a blue plaque above the door of one of its shops.

On several occasions, I had even entered the premises in question, 18 Bolton Street, a jeweller's shop where I go if my watch needs a new battery. How I have missed this plaque, I cannot explain - it is positioned directly over the entrance-door.

At first, I wondered if it had only gone up recently. However, 2006, all of fifteen years ago, is the date registered on the plaque when the Ramsbottom Heritage Society posted it in recognition of a previous occupant going back to the 19th century.

How much longer might this item of historical interest have escaped my notice if it hadn't been for lockdown? For it was only during one of a series of walks that my wife Anna and I embarked on during this period, with no ulterior aim beyond taking exercise and passing the time of day, that we happened upon the object in question.

Anyway, on the day in question, having overcome initial surprise, we were curious to read the inscription. The name PETER MURRAY McDOUALL was spelt out in broad, imposing letters and, added to it, the dates he lived from 1814 to 1854.

With no serious mathematical skills needed, the immediate conclusion to be drawn was that, whoever he was, his time on earth had not been long. Then to wonder how much he must have packed into the limited number of years that should warrant commemoration over 150 years later.

Hoping for an explanation, we learnt McDouall 'practised medicine in Ramsbottom from 1835-1842, and was living here in 1842'. At first glance, it didn't seem worthy of blue plaque recognition on the face of it.

Reading on though, it was stated: 'In that year he alleged before a parliamentary committee that the Grant Brothers illegally paid wages in truck and he led the two mile procession that delivered the Chartists' National Petition to Parliament'.

This sounded rather more substantial. As well as his foremost role in this procession, McDouall was cited as a 'Chartist Leader', suggesting he had played a central part in activities over a greater period of time than just 1842. As for Chartism itself, I already knew much about the history of the movement in general terms but was minded to check up on it again when I got back home. Also to see if I could find out how the Ramsbottom doctor became so heavily involved. The 'gist' of Chartism was that it had sought by various means to influence the Government of the day to agree to give everyone the right to vote – universal suffrage – at a time when the political system only allowed a few privileged citizens such entitlement. However, it was the precise role that McDouall played that I had suddenly become interested to learn more about.

∞

Mention of the Grant Brothers on the plaque struck a more immediate chord. I'd lived in the town of Ramsbottom long enough to have gained a strong impression that this family, famously associated with the early days of the growth of the cotton industry in the area, had been well regarded. For example, there are a lot of existing place-names to-day called after them such as The Grants, Grants Lane and Grants Wood.

Received wisdom about the Grant Brothers was that they were revered as benevolent factory-owners. As well as seeking to make their business profitable, they were generally considered to have kept the welfare of their workers close to heart. Their reputation had been cemented through the 'identification' of William and Daniel Grant with the Cheeryble Brothers, Charles and Ned - fictional characters in Charles Dickens' late-1830s novel *Nicholas Nickleby*.

At some time in the past, I remembered reading extracts from a biography of the Grants written by the Reverend William Hume Elliot, who had served as a clergyman in Ramsbottom in later years of the 19th century, long after these two Grant brothers had died. I recalled how persuasive Hume Elliot had sounded in demonstrating the link between the Grants and the Cheeryble characters.

With the image of most big businessmen of the 19th century tarnished by comparisons to the miserly Ebenezer Scrooge from *A Christmas Carol*, what an accolade it must have been for the Grants that two family-members had appeared to have been portrayed as relative paragons of virtue in *Nicholas Nickleby*. [1]

∞

However, from the evidence over the door of the jeweller's shop, the Grant Brothers were being depicted in a rather less flattering light. It was clear that Doctor Peter Murray McDouall had given damaging evidence against the Grants to a parliamentary committee, alleging they were acting illegally by not paying their workers proper wages but 'in truck', which meant in tokens or goods instead of coins of the realm. Checking up on the matter later in the day, it appeared that this practice had been banned by an 1831 Act of Parliament.

What substance was there to these allegations and what were the outcomes? Admittedly, only so much detail could have been squeezed on to a plaque this size but surely there were other means of finding answers to questions. On the basis that the Ramsbottom Heritage Society had been responsible for the plaque going up in 2006, perhaps there were articles in past magazines of theirs on the subject? [2] In addition, what could be unearthed about McDouall's involvement with Chartism, both in Ramsbottom and on a broader, national scale? [3]

Coming down from Scotland to set up his practice in Ramsbottom in 1835, life as a doctor had opened his eyes to problems he saw all around him in terms of the poor standard of health of working people. McDouall felt a need to address the general situation in ways that went beyond day-to-day treatment of patients and down to the root causes of often shocking levels of hardship. Almost straightaway, he laid blame at the door of the factory system and the merciless way in which it was operated.

However, tackling the situation was another matter. Even if there were many workers who would have been grateful for what he set out to do on their behalf, people in positions of authority, such as the factory-owners themselves, did not thank him for what they saw as meddling interference.

∞

For the truth was that, in purely economic terms, the factory system was proving an outstanding success. As far as the Government was concerned, its development had been a key factor in the country's ground-breaking Industrial Revolution, putting Britain on a pedestal as the 'workshop of the world'. No matter that all the financial benefits accrued to a rising breed of industrial entrepreneurs, based in fast-growing northern towns - looking to make massive profits for themselves whilst paying minimal wages to their workers - amongst whom the Grant Brothers might have been cited as prominent examples.

Without the protection of trade unions, the work-force had been constrained to endure threateningly harsh labour and living conditions. In fact, any attempt made by workers to formally discuss matters amongst themselves was heavily censured by law. In 1834, for example, six labourers - who came to be known as the Tolpuddle Martyrs – ended up being transported to Australia for doing nothing more serious than swearing a secret oath as members of the Friendly Society of Agricultural Labourers. Meanwhile, those in authority stubbornly kept turning a blind eye to the ever greater hardships being suffered by the working population.

Mindful of wanting to do his best to find ways to address issues, McDouall would hardly have needed reminding that the problems went back long before his own time. Other individuals and groups of people had already sought to take action to support a working population that regularly struggled to make ends meet. Knowing this would not have made it any easier but only lent an added edge of frustration. Up as far as the 1830s, the main means of protest undertaken had been through meetings, marches and petitions. Invariably though, reformers had come up against the repressive reaction of a Government implacably set against the notion of any radical re-shaping of society or methods of working.

∞

Plaque Two: The Chatterton Riot of 1826

Many East Lancashire inhabitants, living in the first half of the 19th century, had strong cause to recall various episodes in previous years that highlighted the merciless attitude meted out by authority even to those assembling to make peaceful protest. A strong degree of lingering discontent on this score must have been apparent to a newcomer like McDouall arriving on the local scene in 1835.

By way of broader context, after the battle of Waterloo in 1815 and the end of the Napoleonic Wars, there had followed a particularly severe economic slump leading to harvest failure and chronic unemployment levels. Adding insult to injury, the Government had passed a Corn Law in 1815 which deliberately set out to protect rich home landowners against cheaper foreign corn inputs, thereby forcing working people to pay higher prices for staple food such as bread.

At this time, only around 11 percent of adult males were eligible to vote, very few of whom lived in the industrial north, which was worst hit by deteriorating economic conditions. More enlightened reformers had taken the view that the situation could only be addressed properly if the working class was enfranchised and granted the right to vote. Then there would be a much better chance of acts passed by Parliament serving the interests of the majority of people as opposed to just a privileged few. Instigating a mass campaign to lobby parliament in favour of full manhood suffrage, reformers had gained three-quarters of a million signatures on a petition drawn up during the course of 1817, but the document was flatly rejected by the House of Commons.

When a second slump had occurred in 1819, protesters had sought to mobilise huge crowds in an effort to try again to persuade the government to acknowledge the need for reform. With the north-west being the hub of the movement, a mass rally had been arranged to take place at St Peter's Field, Manchester, on 16 August 1819, with a leading address to be given by well-known radical orator Henry Hunt.

Shortly after the meeting began, local magistrates called upon the Manchester and Salford Yeomanry to arrest Hunt and others on the platform with him. In the course of what followed, eighteen protesters had been killed, with hundreds more seriously injured, after cavalry had charged into the crowd of around 60,000 people who had gathered to lobby for wider electoral representation. The event was assigned the evocative description that would endure - the 'Peterloo Massacre' - by the radical Manchester Observer newspaper in a bitterly ironic reference to the bloody Battle of Waterloo that had taken place four years earlier.

Although all London and regional newspapers shared the horror felt in the Manchester region, the Government's own unrepentant reaction, on the back of what had happened, was to pass the 'Six Acts', which were aimed at suppressing any further meetings in future convened for the purpose of advancing the cause of radical reform.

∞

Another strong sense of grievance amongst workers stemmed from the fact that newly-invented machinery provided an added threat to their job security.

I was reminded of when Anna and I had first been searching in 1996 for a house in the local area. We had viewed a property at '12 Chatterton', situated close to the Stubbins road going out of Ramsbottom towards Edenfield. The occupiers, in the course of showing us around, made reference in hushed tones to 'murderous deeds' perpetrated on this same site in the early nineteenth century. Exchanging glances, we tried to work out whether the story was intended as selling-point or sympathetically-offered deterrent.

What we learnt was that, in the year 1826, the so-called 'Chatterton Riot' took place, coinciding with a time of economic hardship when workers also very much feared the extent to which new labour-saving inventions were costing them their jobs. On 26 April 1826, a large group of workers from across East Lancashire, estimated on the day to be between 3 to 4,000 in number, had made its way from Rawtenstall to Edenfield intent on destroying factory power looms.

The soldiers of the 60th Rifle Corps had been called to Chatterton to deal with the situation. William Grant (one of the Grant family already mentioned), also went out to the scene in his capacity as a local Justice of the Peace. Appealing for calm, Grant asked the crowd to disperse but to no avail. At this point, he had read out the 'Riot Act'. This meant that any actions the crowd now took could be construed as a felony, punishable by death. Rashly, the crowd not only failed to disperse but set about invading Chatterton Mill. One man's statement gave an indication of the desperate mood of the crowd when he shouted, 'I'd rather be killed on this spot than go home and starve. I'm not leaving this place until every loom is destroyed.' [4]

This is in fact what happened next but not without retribution from the Rifle Corps. With the crowd attempting a mass exodus from the scene, having done the damage they had come to inflict, a few of those fleeing sought refuge on the premises of 12 Chatterton. A group of soldiers had caught up with them though, ending in the killing of four men and one woman. A fifth man, an innocent onlooker by the name of James Waddicar, who was concerned on the day for the welfare of his neighbour, Betty Upton, was also killed. In all, 42 'rioters' were arrested. They were tried at assizes set up at The Horse and Jockey Inn in nearby Edenfield. Initially, every one of them was sentenced to death before being told their sentences had been commuted to transportation to Australia.

Despite all the gruesome reported happenings, Anna and I had ended up buying 12 Chatterton. Intent on finding out more about the history connected to it, we discovered in due course where the nearby Chatterton Mill would have been situated (owned at the time by Thomas Aitken). The mill had long since vanished. The site it once occupied became a public park in the course of time which 12 Chatterton now looks out onto across a narrow laneway. How deceptively peaceful the whole setting appears in modern times. It is extremely difficult to imagine that any industrial activity, let alone such a horrific event could have taken place in this sleepy-looking location.

We had moved out of 12 Chatterton in 2000. Recently, more than twenty years later, also by chance during lockdown, we thought one day to take a walk down through Stubbins to Chatterton and found ourselves taking another look at the house we had lived in for four years. Feeling a sense of nostalgia, wandering by the property, it still looked exactly the same in every respect - except for one additional feature - namely, the blue plaque that had since been placed on the front wall of the house by the Edenfield Local History Society in 2003.

Irrespective of the tragic details the plaque unfolded, the justification for having attached it to the front wall of 12 Chatterton seemed entirely worthy, commemorating as it did those lives that had been so cruelly taken there on 26 April 1826.

∞

Plaque Three: John Kay

Given that one of the main causes leading up to the 'Chatterton Riot' had been the introduction of labour-saving devices in cotton-mills, it is worth saying that this was no new phenomenon at the time, such a trend having started well before the 19th century. From the very beginning, factory-owners had kept a sharp eye out for any savings to be made and were grateful for any technological advances that cut production costs. Sometimes though, looking at it from the point of view of inventors themselves, even the most effective inventions they managed to devise often failed to accrue personal financial profit.

I was to come upon an illustration of this on making a visit to Park House, a local residence only half a mile or so from where we now live on Bury New Road in Ramsbottom. On this occasion, in February 2021, I took the chance to view a plaque put up by the

Metropolitan Borough of Bury in commemoration of the fact it was 'in this house John Kay, Inventor of the Flying Shuttle, was born 17 July 1704'. [5]

By way of background, John's father, Robert, had been a yeoman farmer owning the surrounding Park Estate in Walmersley. John, born in 1704 and fifth son out of ten children overall, was somewhat towards the back of the family inheritance queue. It might have seemed a blessing to him that, from an early age, he was drawn more towards engineering than agriculture as a future career.

In practical terms, he was to prove very successful in his chosen pursuit. After all, he was to establish himself as a pioneer inventor in the great age of technological advance in the cotton manufacturing industry that would continue through the 18th century. Further inventions were to follow on with James Hargreaves' Spinning Jenny (1764), Richard Arkwright's Water Frame (1769), Samuel Crompton's Mule (1775) and Edmund Cartwright's Power Loom (1784).

Kay's Flying Shuttle revolutionised the weaving process in terms both of speed and economy of operation. Only half the labour was now needed compared with before. Understandably though, this had not gone down well with workers who, never mind the genius element to the invention, saw it starkly for what it was: a direct threat to their economic livelihood.

In the end, John Kay might have wished he had stayed on in Walmersley and stuck to the rural way of life. Ultimately, he was to fall victim to both industrialists and workers. For in those early days, inventors like Kay were to learn the hard way that it was not enough to come up with a prototype device but equally important to secure the patent. Sold short by factory-owners and hounded by resentful workers, Kay had ended up in 1747 fleeing to France. Occasionally, he braved it back to England only to find himself even more unpopular than ever for the fact his invention had continued to cause ever-increasing levels of unemployment. On one occasion in 1753, it was said that he was in his Bury home when it was broken into by a mob and that he had only narrowly escaped with his life. Kay died in France in 1779, by most accounts alone and penniless.

It was not until very much later in time that John Kay's achievements as an inventor were to gain any sort of formal recognition. Indeed not until the start of the 20th century. In 1903, it was felt that Bury 'owed John Kay's memory an atonement', and that all Bury should contribute in restitution to 'that wonderfully ingenious and martyred man'. Kay Gardens and the Kay Monument were opened in Bury in 1908.

Apart from any other lessons to be learnt from John Kay's story, the main one was that anyone hoping to make their fortune in the burgeoning cotton industry of the day needed above all else to adopt a hard-headed, pragmatic business approach if they were to have any chance of achieving financial success.

∞

Plaque Four: The Grants

It is the year 1783 when the Grants first enter upon the local scene. The family's rags-to-riches story epitomises the way in which it was possible through grit and determination, even during hard times, to overcome obstacles in life such as poverty and hardship.

A blue plaque commemorating this illustrious family in Ramsbottom's history is attached to the front of a building in the centre of town, at 'Top o' the Brow' in Ramsbottom Square. The building, now corporately known as 'The Grants' was the site of 'The Grant Arms Hotel', until the premises recently changed hands to become the local headquarters of the business-firm, Rosebridge.

Also put in place by the Ramsbottom Heritage Society, in 2007, the plaque cites that this marks the spot where, from 1806, 'William and Grace had once lived'. Mention is then made, in time-honoured fashion, of the link between their sons William and Daniel and the Cheeryble Brothers in Charles Dickens' novel, *Nicholas Nickleby*. Certain other information is contained on the plaque but, as said in relation to the one commemorating Peter Murray McDouall on nearby Bolton Street, only so much detail can be covered in the space permitted.

The story of the Grant family, from before the time they arrived in East Lancashire in 1783 and thereafter, is one proudly told by biographer William Hume Elliot, 'Ramsbottom's first historian'. Much of his account was based on documents written retrospectively towards the end of his life by William Grant, son of William and Grace.

In 1783, father William Grant (born 1733) and Grace (born 1743), had been living in poverty as farmers in the Highlands of Scotland suffering in the midst of a protracted economic depression. Together, they had made a life-changing decision to uproot and embark on a 300-mile journey to Manchester. The idea had come to William who, from previous experience of travelling south of the border driving cattle to market, had heard of jobs going in the expanding cotton industry in Lancashire. [6]

Between them, believing they had to make the switch for the sake of the family's future, William and Grace had sold up everything they had to finance this giant trek. Everything that is except for their horse and cart, which they needed to transport themselves and seven children. Banking on gaining employment in Manchester, William carried in his pocket a letter of introduction to Richard Arkwright who had just opened a factory there and was apparently keen to recruit workers.

Most of the roads in Scotland at that time only amounted to rough tracks. Up to crossing the English border, their progress had been agonisingly slow. By comparison, things seemed to speed up a bit after reaching Carlisle. Then beyond that: Skipton and Burnley. From there, they passed through the Lancashire villages of Crawshawbooth, Rawtenstall, Haslingden, Edenfield and Shuttleworth. At a point just beyond Shuttleworth, on the Manchester Road leading to Bury and very close to the Kay family's Park Farm Estate, they decided to rest for the night.

By this stage, the family's situation had become desperate. Without a penny left to them, during that evening they had eaten their last remaining food. For weeks, they had been living off the cakes Grace had baked back in Scotland - 'bannocks' made out of oatmeal - which it had been hoped would last them the journey. Now though, starvation stared them in the face, both without food of their own or means of buying it. With their backs to the wall, that night the Grants spent a long time praying to God for deliverance from the plight they found themselves in.

Despite everything, William is said to have gone into raptures about the view they had from the hillside. Looking down from on high, he caught sight of the tiny hamlet of Ramsbottom below with the River Irwell flowing through it. Nostalgic for what he had left behind in Scotland, William paid the highest compliment he could to the view by saying the look of the River Irwell reminded him of his beloved River Spey back in the Highlands. Certainly William and Grace's children – those old enough at the time to remember – made this episode an integral part of the Grant folklore which they would 'nae let be forgotten'!

Although they knew they needed to set out as early as possible the next morning to make it to Manchester, the memory of this briefest of stays was to stay vividly in their minds. It was also to determine in later life how the Grant children would decide to honour the memory of their parents in the special way they did.

∞

At this stage, it may be helpful to introduce the seven children accompanying their parents. After all, what they were to accomplish in later life was very much to characterise the industrial environment of Ramsbottom that McDouall encountered on arrival in 1835.

In order of seniority, as quoted in a passage taken from Hume Elliot, they were:

'James, baptised 1768 and about 15 years old;
William, baptised 1769 and about 14 years old;
Elizabeth, baptised 1773 and about 10 years old;
John, baptised 1775 and about 8 years old;
Mary, baptised 1777 and about 6 years old;
Isabella, baptised 1780 and about 3 years old;
Donald (Daniel), baptised 1783 and about six months old'. [7]

Apart from all other hazards parents William and Grace would have faced to this point in their journey, the sheer size, as well as the assortment of young ages, of their family must have added considerably to the scale and pressures of the whole venture.

Early as the family had intended setting off the following morning, they were to be delayed by the unexpected arrival on the scene of two local men stopping them in their tracks. Apparently, these two had got up at the crack of dawn with the purpose of hunting for food in the area.

Despite this original 'game-plan', the curiosity of the two had been taken by the wholly strange scene they had come across at 'The Top o' th' Hoof' ('Hoof' meaning steep hill). In particular, they had been taken aback by the broad accent with which they heard the woman addressing the man, whom they rightly assumed to be her husband, which came across to their ears as a wild-sounding foreign language. [8]

What understandably took the hunting pair even more by surprise though was the large number of young children the couple had in tow. Wiping their eyes and re-counting, they ended up at seven. Supposing this throng were travelling any kind of distance, how exactly could all nine of them have managed to fit into this single horse and cart contraption in the first place?

Even if it meant putting off their hunting activities for a short while, what harm could there have been in taking a bit of time out to satisfy their curiosity as to what this incongruous-looking bunch of people was doing here in the first place?

An hour later, 'William's frank and manly answers to the questions and the strangely pathetic picture before their eyes, so impressed them that they thrust two sovereigns into his hand, and, bidding him good morning and better luck, with moistened eyes and quickened step hastened from the scene'. As Hume Elliot continues, 'One regrets that it is not known who these singularly timely and generous benefactors were'. [9]

Freed in this way from their state of penury, the family pushed on through Bury to Manchester, a distance of twelve miles. However, upon reaching their final destination, William was to suffer what might have seemed the ultimate setback to his hopes and aspirations upon discovering that Mr. Arkwright had so many applications to hand that he was in no position to employ another single worker.

∞

Lesser spirits might have found this a crushing blow but William persevered and his resilience was to be rewarded. Offers of work came in for the elder boys James and William from a fellow-countryman, mill-owner Mr. James Dinwiddie, whom William Grant had known from earlier days back in Scotland.

Hampson Mill, about a mile and a half south of Bury, specialised in calico printing. The apprenticeship the Grant children served in this branch of the cotton industry was to stand them in good stead in their own later careers as factory-owners. Dinwiddie also found employment for John and Elizabeth. Further than this, he provided a cottage for the family to live in, which although described as 'humble', at least gave them a roof over their heads for the time being.

While they were living in this cottage at Haslam Bank, on the southern fringe of Bury, Hume Elliot describes how 'a great never-forgotten family sorrow befell them'. Through misadventure, daughter Mary on a stormy day somehow had ended up being 'blown into the nearby river'. Her body was buried at Bank Street cemetery with her tombstone bearing the following inscription:-

'Here resteth, in the hope of a blessed resurrection,
Mary, the daughter of William Grant
Of Strathspey, North Britain,
Who died the 13th day of November, 1784,
In the 8th year of her age'.

By way of trying to overcome this tragedy, the Grants threw themselves even harder into their work. In the course of time, James, William and John had finished their apprenticeships while Daniel entered upon his, also at Hampson Mill. Then it occurred to the family to try and build up a business of their own.

They moved house from Haslam Bank to Bury Lane, a better-class business and residential district of Bury. There they sold linen, cloth and prints. Not long after, though, they were moving on again after taking up new business premises in the Wylde, then known as the Market Place, in the centre of town.

The often-called 'rags to riches' story of the Grants was perceived to have come about as a result of solid effort, characterised by long years of conducting business along hard-headed and pragmatic lines. With eldest brother James returning to Scotland to set up his own business in Glasgow, it was second son William who became the family's fulcrum. As for father William Grant, 50 years old when first coming down here from Scotland, he increasingly took a back seat.

Not perhaps surprisingly, it had been William senior who had encountered most difficulty coming to terms with the demands of the Lancashire factory system. With so much of his earlier life having been spent in the open-air style of Highland existence, he hadn't found it easy to adapt. Arriving at a kind of compromise, he had ended up opening a mobile market of his own trading in 'fents' – off-cut cotton items of clothing – enabling him to travel around East Lancashire selling goods to interested customers. At the same time, he would no doubt have taken consolation from the fact his children proved capable of coping with the rigours of the factory system.

He and Grace must have felt very proud of the progress made over time by their children within this new industrial climate. Talking of off-spring, the Grant family had been added to with the birth of Charles in 1788.

One of the major stepping-stones for the Grants – apart from 'ceaseless activity and long hours' - was an ever strengthening link with the firm of Messrs. Peel (father of the famous Prime Minister-to-be) and Yates who were well-established as factory-owners in Bury since 1770, branching out to Ramsbottom in 1783.

'William Grant and Brothers', as the Grant family firm came to be known, was eventually to buy Peel and Yates' Ramsbottom 'Old Ground' Print Works off them in 1806. Not content with this, the Grants purchased Nuttall Mill in 1812 and later the Park Estate in 1827.

With this latter acquisition, it must have given the Grant family tremendous satisfaction realising they had completely 'turned round' that day in 1783 when the family had felt so much on the verge of despair on their seemingly never-ending journey down from Scotland.

Dying in 1817, William Grant senior did not live to see the moment when everything that had captured his imagination back then in 1783 – that is, the spectacular view looking down to the river-valley below – had now come to be owned by the family. Grace died four years after him in 1821. Elizabeth had died previously in 1808. They had been laid to rest in Bank Street cemetery beside Mary.

Since 1806, after first coming to live in Ramsbottom, William and Grace had resided, as stated on the plaque, in the building called 'Top o' th' Brow', standing at the upper end of Bridge Street. Grace loved cultivating flowers and plants and her garden was noted for being heart-shaped.

Not so long after the two of them had passed away, the present frontage, very much still visible to-day, was added to with the premises coming into being as 'The Grant Arms Hotel' from 1828 onwards.

∞

Grants Tower

As mentioned previously, the Grant family never allowed it to slip from memory how, on their epic journey from Scotland, they had spent that evening hunkering down in the open air on a raw hillside overlooking the Ramsbottom river-valley below.

Over fifty years later, in tribute to the memory of their parents, the wealthy remaining off-spring of parents, William and Grace, decided to build 'Grants Tower', a four-storey stone construction, in the wild and remote location of Top o' th' Hoof, high above the road connecting Bury and Rawtenstall. The aim was for this magnificent edifice to stand out on the horizon, capturing the same stunning view of the valley as father William had first glimpsed in 1783.

∞

On another of our local walks, this one taking place in March 2021, Anna and I had climbed up Bury New Road from our present house and then, reaching the top, turned right along the old Bury road. Walking past Park House and Park Farm Garden Centre and café on either side, we knew we must be getting close to the point where we would have to ascend another even steeper hill in order to locate Grants Tower.

Despite understanding that it had originally been built to command the horizon, there was no visible sign today of any such edifice from the road below. At first, we supposed it could be down to the shielding woodland that has enveloped the hills over the last 200 years or so.

A helpful-sounding clue we had been given was to look for a telecommunications mast as a point of direction. Thankfully, for the purposes of the exercise, this gaunt modern construction was strikingly in view. Relieved on this score, we marched on up the hill.

Eventually, despite one or two wrong turns, we finally managed to come across what we were looking for. Alas though, it has to be said, nowhere near the grand four-storey edifice of old.

From what remains of the 'Tower' today, it requires a considerable feat of imagination to try and reconstruct in the mind what it would have looked like when it was built in 1829. On completion, the records show that, standing 800 feet above sea level, it would have been a 50 feet high, four-storey structure with four flights of stairs, 84 individual steps and eight turrets at the top, two of which were disguised chimneys for fireplaces below.

Thankfully, we had not allowed ourselves to expect too much on arrival! Prey to the foulest of weather conditions and having suffered long years of neglect, the once-imposing edifice had finally collapsed and been reduced to rubble in 1944. [10]

Encouragingly though, some recent restoration has been carried out on the original site. Certain stonework has been sorted, cleaned and put back into place at ground floor level by current owner of the land, Mr Buckley. A zinc roof has been installed to prevent the risk of further damage from the elements. The building though is never likely again to re-capture the height and splendour of its former glory.

Apart from being a shrine to their parents, Grants Tower had originally been built to be lived in as a house, even if this turned out not to be members of the Grant family themselves. There had been one or two occupiers with a distinctive story of their own to be told, including steeplejack James Duncan Wright and poet Edwin Waugh. [11]

Another benefit of the restoration work is that it serves to attract people to visit this remote point on a hillside when otherwise they might have no reason to do so. Irrespective of the scale of work which would be needed to restore it fully, no-one could fail to find the view across the valley from this landmark as captivating to the senses as William Grant senior had once done.

∞

There is no question of the hugely important role played by the Grant family in the unfolding history of Ramsbottom up to the time and beyond when Peter Murray McDouall started up his medical practice in 1835. By this point, they had become by far the most prominent factory- and property-owners in the local area. They were at the height of their powers, including wielding considerable civic influence, with family lynchpin William serving as Justice of the Peace.

It is into this setting that McDouall arrives (he too coming from Scotland) intent on ministering to the health and well-being of the local population. On the face of things, there was no reason to think he would experience too much difficulty in adapting to his new surroundings.

However, it was soon to become clear, especially as far as the Grants were concerned, that here was an idealistic young man cherishing principles which would cause him to take issue with the way they were accustomed to running their business.

The Grants espoused the factory system as a way of maximising economic output while at the same time feeling they honoured their side of the commercial bargain by paying decent wages and arranging to put a roof over workers' heads.

Not requiring anyone to look too closely under the surface of such dealings, the Grants were unlikely to thank McDouall for raising matters of concern he might have, let alone addressing them to others in public forums. Nor were they likely to have much sympathy with the broader radical views he expressed.

Over the next few years, motivated by quite different sets of values and priorities, the Grants and young Doctor McDouall found themselves inevitably headed on a collision course.

NOTES ON SOURCES

1. The Reverend William Hume Elliot (1837-1927) first came to Ramsbottom in 1874 to take up post as a pastor until eventually retiring from the ministry in 1907. During this time, he wrote two biographies of the Grants, firstly *The Country and Church of the Cheeryble Brothers* (George Lewis and Son, Selkirk, 1893) which was followed by *The Story of the Cheeryble Grants* (Sherratt and Hughes, Manchester, 1906). The books overlap quite a lot in content. What is particularly useful in the first is the wealth of detail provided on how Ramsbottom had developed as a town during the early decades of the 19th century. The second book, which the author dedicated to the Dickens Fellowship, concentrates more specifically on the lives of brothers William and Daniel, providing additional information accumulated from 1893 onwards with a view, it appears, to seeking to strengthen the Cheeryble link and thereby the brothers' notable reputation.

   If the brothers are seen as having any less than perfect traits in their character, the author invariably finds a redeeming explanation. As for mention of McDouall, Hume Elliot makes only one passing reference to him, (on page 136 of *The Country and Church of the Cheeryble Brothers* - albeit misspelling his name 'McDougal'), as one of the 'radicals' living in Ramsbottom in the late 1830s.

2. An article by Andrew Todd (RHS Magazine No. 23 Spring 2002 pp. 11-20) - *George Goodrick, the Grant Arms and the Truck System* - was to prove particularly valuable as a means of learning about local issues leading to McDouall giving evidence against the Grants to Parliament in 1842. The implications raised by this article will be examined in detail in a later chapter. An article which was helpful in establishing the profile of McDouall in broader terms was one written by Trevor Park (RHS Magazine No. 7 Summer 1993 pp.9-11) – *The Mysterious Doctor McDouall.*

Another intriguing article, written by Andrew Todd (RHS Magazine No. 25 Autumn 2003 pp. 1-12) is *Peter Murray McDouall, Charles Dickens and the Grant Myth*. Here, the author sets out to show that, despite Hume Elliot's glorification of the Grants as models for Dickens' Cheeryble Brothers, McDouall had revealed a different side of them in a way that brought the 'Grant Myth' into question. Reading this article certainly provided a launching-pad for seeking to address the matter in greater depth as to how and why McDouall took such exception to the Grants.

3. Starting out by looking for contemporary 19th century accounts, the first one I came across - in the Tameside Local Studies and Archives Centre in Ashton-under-Lyne - was Robert George Gammage's *History of the Chartist Movement 1837-1853*, originally published in 1854 with a second revised edition in 1894. Born in 1821 in Northampton, he was, like McDouall, a doctor by profession who was also destined to take an active role in supporting Chartism. Gammage appears to have known McDouall well. This comes across in the first-hand accounts he provides of his fellow doctor's involvement in the movement. More reference will be made to Gammage and Chartist historians, writing later, in subsequent chapters.

4. Finding a copy of John Simpson's *A History of Edenfield and District* (published by Edenfield Local History Society in 2003) in the Archive section of Bury Library proved valuable in tracking down the detail of events taking place at Chatterton in 1826 (pp 46-48)

5. John Kay's is the only plaque of the four put up in a setting away from public view. I had needed to ask permission before entering the private premises of Park House to go and read the inscription which was visible on a side of the house looking out over a stretch of garden. I had made my request to view the plaque to Judith and Kathryn, who run the Park Farm Tea

Room across the way from Park House. As well as having a chance to go over the road to see the plaque, I was interested in reading some of the history, up on the walls of the tearoom, regarding how John Lees and his family, from the late 1950s onwards, had carved out an up-to-date Park Farm business, connecting up a garden-centre, the tearooms, a shop and an outside contracting service.

In addition to the Kay plaque, other information, carved into stone on the same stretch of wall, told how Park House had been 're-built for John and Margaret Lees & Family by Andrew Manley 1998'. It was interesting to sight another inscription on the same wall reading as follows:

The Lees Family:
Joan Margaret 1958
Sandra Elizabeth 1960
Judith Ann 1964
John Edward 1966
Kathryn Sarah 1969
Susan Barbara 1971.

Incidentally, from details mounted on the walls of the Tea Room, it was interesting to learn that, apart from the entrepreneurial prowess the family had demonstrated over recent decades, they had also won fame on a televised, national level. In 2007, sisters Sandra, Judith and Susan, together with friend Justine, had pulled off a major culinary coup by winning a competition (against stiff opposition, having to serve up 50 starters, 50 main courses and 50 desserts), hosted and organised by celebrity chef Gordon Ramsay at his Claridge's 'F-Word' restaurant in London!

6. An earlier episode in the life of William senior, which son William didn't appear too keen to relay, was his father's

involvement at the age of 13 (together with his elder brothers Alexander and Daniel) in the 1746 Battle of Culloden.

Despite the Chief of the Grant Clan declaring in favour of the ruling British King George II, the three Grant brothers joined the ranks of the opposing army led by the so-called 'Young Pretender', Bonnie Prince Charlie, the Scots-affiliated claimant to King George's throne.

The story of William senior's role, on the losing side and subsequently harried by the king's soldiers, is described by Brenda Richards (RHS Magazine No. 34 Spring 2008 pp. 20) – *The Grants at the Battle of Culloden*.

7. Hume Elliot took this detail from 'the register of the parish of Knockando' in the Scottish Highlands. He went on to add though that the register may somehow have listed Isabella and Daniel the wrong way round. The evidence which Hume Elliot uses to show that this might well have been the case is that, when Daniel eventually died in 1855, his 'memorial tablet' recorded him as being 'aged 75 years'. In addition, by way of clarifying the apparent anomaly of Daniel being named 'Donald' at his baptism, Hume Elliot adds that 'to this day Donald and Daniel are often regarded in the North as synonymous'.

What else do we learn from Hume Elliot about the Grant children from the times before they arrived in Lancashire in 1783? Being the two eldest, James and William had served stints as apprentice shepherds. Then there is the account of how William had tragically lost the use of one eye after 'a servant girl very fond of him snatched him up one day and danced round the kitchen with him in her arms. But, unfortunately, she slipped, and the little fellow's face fell on the embers on the hearth. Rescue was the work of a moment, but, unhappily, one eye was destroyed'. (*The Story of the Cheeryble Grants* p. 126). From this time, William had a glass eye which was said to have wobbled in its socket on occasions when his facial expression may uncharacteristically have become more animated.

8. To appreciate just how difficult it would have been for our two local game-hunters to understand what Grace might have been saying to her husband, the following is a passage which Hume Elliot (he too was from a Scottish background and was expert in a range of local dialects) incorporated into his book to highlight the distinctive nature of the Highland vernacular. The passage in question (*The Story of the Cheeryble Grants* p. 73) reveals Grace reporting how her Highland friends had stated their apprehension to her about making the hazardous long journey to 'Lankishire' in the first place. 'Translations' are provided in brackets:

'Ye'll get dune for, wumman, or droned, or be fund streckit (stretched out) ahint some auld fail-dyke (turf-wall), afore ye get tae the Lowthians, let alane that Lankishire. It's fair waesome (woeful)! An' a pether (pedlar) telt me, the folk thereawa' wear airn shune (iron-shoes, clogs), an' kick for daffin (diversion)! Gaun a'the gate there – an' tae sic clanjamfrie (undesirable people), wi' a' their graceless gilraivery (riotous conduct)? It's a dillabaleerie (nonsense)!'

Facing such reservations, Grace had dismissed them in the end as 'clishmaclaverin' - translated as 'silly, idle talk bandied about' - demonstrating the strong-mindedness she was always noted for. The Grant children always maintained that it was their mother who had been the family's principal driving-force.

9. Hume Elliot, *The Story of the Cheeryble Grants* pp 84-5.

10. Dwelling on the subject of towers in the area, of course the Peel Monument now dominates the skyline on its own. Built in 1852 to honour local Bury-born Prime Minister Robert Peel - son of the Robert Peel who had sold his factory in Ramsbottom to the Grants in 1806 - it meant that, until the collapse of Grants Tower in 1944, there had been two tall towers staring at one

another across the valley. Built on Holcombe Hill, the Peel Monument stands 1,100 feet above sea level and is 128 feet high. More mention will be made later of the circumstances behind the erection of this tower.

11. Local historian Chris Aspin's work *The Fastest Man: Steeple Jack's Adventures in Lancashire* (2009) - copy in the Archive section of Bury Library - tells the life of James Duncan Wright, born in Dundee in 1829, who came to live in Grants Tower in the 1850s while working in Lancashire. Wright had first come to the attention of the Grants when they had needed someone to repair a factory chimney of theirs in Ramsbottom. Apart from a natural expertise in carrying out work at considerable height, his methods were extremely unorthodox. Ignoring more conventional methods involving ladders or scaffolding, he adopted a system of 'flying ropes' that he reputedly swung up and down on at levels of speed reaching 100 miles an hour. On the back of such feats, he had been given the nickname 'Steeple Jack', a term which has now become part of the English language.

Meanwhile, Rochdale-born Edwin Waugh (1817-1890) was a dialect poet, sometimes referred to as the Lancashire Robert Burns.

A source providing encouragement for people to walk up to what remains of Grants Tower is Andrew Gill's recently-published *Victorian Rossendale Walks: The End of an Era.* The underlying thread behind this book is to recreate the interest the Rev. James Marshall Mather (1851-1916) had taken during the late 19th century tracking various paths across the Rossendale district; having published two compilations of local walks himself in 1888 and 1894.

CHAPTER TWO

The Radical Upbringing of
Peter Murray McDouall.

Twenty-one years of age when he arrived in Ramsbottom in 1835, Peter Murray McDouall had every good reason to hope for a long career ahead of him as a doctor. On his way down from Scotland, (it had been nothing like as long and hazardous a journey as that of the Grants fifty years earlier) he had spent a brief spell carrying out certain medical duties in Burnley before starting up his practice on Bolton Street.

Born in 1814 in Newton Stewart, in the county of Wigtownshire in Scotland, McDouall was venturing into entirely new territory in coming to Lancashire. Even so, it would have been encouraging, knowing how commonly Scots like himself had managed to migrate south to these parts and adapt successfully to a new life. Not only had his fellow-countrymen, although seen as outsiders, generally been well-accepted but also, in celebrated instances, succeeded in making a prosperous living for themselves. What better example than the Grant Brothers?

Firmly established as factory-owners, the Grants now encouraged fellow-Scots to come to work for them. Not that McDouall had prior connection, let alone any proffered welcome from anyone in the family. However, the extent to which the brothers' 'fame' had spread far and wide may well have acted as a spur to anyone coming from north of the border.

It would have been interesting for McDouall to compare Ramsbottom with Newton Stewart. Over the previous two decades, the Scottish town he had been brought up in had experienced a similar kind of development. At the time of his birth, Newton Stewart had been a quiet spot on the river Cree with little more than a hundred or so inhabitants, a market-centre on the road that stretched from Dumfries to the western port of Stranraer, lying a further 25 miles away from McDouall's home town.

However, this relatively short distance must have provided a strong draw at the time, particularly during spells of economic hardship, for people in the locality to think about perhaps re-locating to nearby Ireland or beyond that, rather more temptingly, across the Atlantic Ocean to the 'new world' of America. Taking the opposite route, it was only 80 miles or so to England and the border city of Carlisle.

From 1815 onwards, Newton Stewart had undergone rapid growth which had seen the town's population rise to over 2,000 by 1835. The fact that this expansion was largely based on the growth of a native cotton industry must have established a further link in the young doctor's mind with how Ramsbottom itself had developed in recent years.

McDouall's knowledge and awareness of workings of the cotton industry back home might have made him curious to see how things operated by comparison in the East Lancashire setting. In Newton Stewart, he had witnessed first-hand the wretched conditions in the factories and the adverse effects this had on the health and well-being of the town's local hand loom weavers, working in conditions of extreme hardship and earning only meagre wages for their toils.

∞

Although there is a considerable amount of evidence available regarding McDouall's life from 1835 onwards, not so much is known about his upbringing in Scotland leading up to the time he ventured to Ramsbottom. [1]

Brought up in what would have been seen at that time as a middle-class family background, Peter received a fairly liberal education at the local school he attended. His father, Andrew, was known locally as 'Will Wander, the poet of the Cree'. What else he did for a living is not clear, but it seems to have been sufficient for the family to accumulate some property and provide young McDouall with a comfortable and secure upbringing. Little at all is known by comparison about his mother or two sisters.

As well as affording him an informed, open-minded attitude to life, Peter grew up in an unusually free-thinking religious environment where the prevailing culture was one of 'dissent' to any practices steeped in dogma. Later in life, he was quoted as saying that he remained a critic of the 'rotten and slimy slough of Churchism, but not of "true religion", and that he continued to "honour and revere Christianity and the Bible" '. [2]

Additional funds for the boy's education accrued from a trust fund set up by his uncle, Peter McDouall, who was the Baillie of Newton Stewart, an office in Scottish local government similar to that of an alderman or magistrate. With this additional backing, he embarked on a medical education, serving a five-year apprenticeship with Mr McMillan, a surgeon in Newton Stewart, before completing his training in Glasgow and Edinburgh. During his period of service in Newton Stewart, he had tended to factory casualties and seen for himself the consequences of cotton industry workers being exposed to perilous conditions with regular risk of and liability to injury and illness.

Alongside wanting to become a doctor, McDouall's outlook appears to have been strongly influenced by his father's standing as a poet. Andrew's soubriquet, 'Will Wander', stemmed from his having produced verse with titles such as *Will Wander of Benarrow's Trip to America*. Son Peter inherited his father's penchant for poetry and would go on to write his own. As well as his father's apparent link with America, stories were handed down to Peter about how his grandfather had fought for the cause of freedom by enlisting in George Washington's army as a soldier serving in the late 18th century American War of Independence. It had a significant effect on Peter, learning that his grandfather had preferred to fight for a cause rather than for country. Later in life, addressing Chartist gatherings, McDouall would proudly commend his grandfather's example as one worthy of emulating in modern times.

∞

The world McDouall grew up in was a volatile one in which the forces for stability and those for change were at constant loggerheads. The outcome of the American War of Independence (1775 to 1783), creating shockwaves across the world, had provided a striking example of the way in which the 'old order' was being taken on and defeated. What was seen as a rough-and-ready bunch of colonial hopefuls had taken on the military might of the British Government and, against all odds, emerged triumphant at the end of an epic conflict on North American soil. A seemingly unthinkable result had been achieved with not only the gaining of separation from Britain but the establishment of a democratic constitution declaring America a free, self-ruling country.

Then, only a few years after, the explosive French Revolution of 1789 had witnessed the people of France rising up against Louis XVI, involving the guillotining of the king and his wife Marie-Antoinette, together with members of their aristocratic entourage who had not managed to flee abroad. Although many people outside France frowned upon what had happened, there were others in Britain, including no doubt the young McDouall, who warmly supported the motives of those who had taken action to assert the right of all people to be granted political representation.

These two seismic events had put repressive governments in other countries into a flat spin, left contemplating the unholy prospect of similar revolutionary activities breaking out in their own backyard. In Britain, measures were quickly taken to clamp down on anything that smacked of popular rebellion.

Punitive measures were carried out, especially against the spread of seditious literature. One particular book, *The Rights of Man* written by Thomas Paine which was published in 1791 and went on to sell over a million copies, clearly supported what had happened in France. The radical views expressed in this book appealed strongly to certain sections of British society such as reformers, Protestant dissenters, London craftsmen and skilled factory hands in the new industrial north of England.

Thomas Paine argued for a redefinition of government in accordance with the American model; the elimination of aristocratic titles; lower taxes for the poor and subsidised education for them. *The Rights of Man* caused a sensation in that it challenged the assumptions upon which the existing British Government operated. Those in authority saw the book as stirring rebellious feelings and inciting revolution. Even though Paine took the precaution of escaping to France, proceedings still went on to try him 'in absentia'. Convicted of seditious libel against the Crown, he was sentenced to hanging. Mindful of self-preservation, Paine stayed on in France and never returned to England, dying of a natural death aged 72 in 1809.

Meanwhile, the impact of what had taken place in France showed no signs of abating. Ironically, having been freed from monarchy, an even more authoritarian dictatorship had emerged. If anything, the fact that a personality such as Napoleon Bonaparte could transcend himself from comparatively humble origins to becoming a virtually self-elected Emperor, proved another wake-up call to the British Government. Bonaparte was further to make his mark by orchestrating a foreign war that lasted more than a decade.

Eventually, the European alliance lined up against Bonaparte, involving Britain, clinched the decisive Battle of Waterloo in 1815. The vanquished Emperor had been packed off in exile to the remote

South Atlantic island of St Helena where he was to die aged 51 in 1821. As soon as possible, European powers, again including Britain, had taken measures to restore the French monarchy, even if for obvious reasons it wasn't Louis XVI himself who took the throne but his Bourbon family-successor, Louis XVIII.

However, it couldn't simply be a case of turning back the clock in France or for that matter in any other country. The central issues, that had sparked two different revolutions, still remained and were not to go away. For example, however much successive English Prime Ministers from 1815 onwards might have liked to see things returning to normal, the lid had been blown off the question of the rights of the so-called 'common people'.

There was always the risk now of comeback if any measures taken to appease the broader populace weren't seen to be going far enough. Bearing such factors in mind, and with the political situation exacerbated by a period of harsh economic conditions, turmoil and unrest was strongly evident across British life during these times.

∞

While revolution was taking hold in certain places abroad, the British Government wrestled with how best to keep control without suffering loss of authority. In the light of this, it is significant to look at the Acts passed by Parliament during the course of these years. The underlying aim, behind every measure that was enacted, was to preserve a society in which the privileged few maintained its traditional power over the masses. Again, it is clear, not least from how McDouall was to react in later years, that he was fundamentally opposed to the repressive effects of so many of the legislative acts passed by the British Government throughout the troubled passage of time that was to follow.

Firstly, in 1815, immediately after the end of the Napoleonic Wars, there had been the Corn Laws, referred to earlier, which imposed a crippling tax on grain imports leaving people having to pay the higher price dictated to them by rich landowners.

The so-called Reform Act of 1832 was seen by many as a belated attempt to address an existing electoral system that was blatantly unfair. However, the right to vote was only extended to the middle-class, including small landowners, tenant farmers, shopkeepers and householders paying a yearly rental of £10 or more. Despite many MPs fearing concessions had gone too far, in reality the Act went no way towards enfranchising the vast majority of potential voters. At that time £10 was not an inconsiderable sum of money. Much as the 1832 Act managed to appease the middle class, the resentment however felt amongst the working class subsequently fuelled the growth of protest movements such as Chartism.

A year after the Reform Act, the government had finally seen fit to try to do something to improve working conditions in factories. Various attempts had ostensibly been made before to impose regulations relating to employment of minors. For example, an 1819 Act of Parliament had stated that, within the cotton industry, no children under 9 years of age were to be employed at all and that the hours worked by children aged 9-16 should be limited to 12 hours per day.

Nevertheless, opinion would have remained very much divided at the time, even on an issue like this. The Grant brothers would probably have argued it hadn't done them any harm working those longer hours they had put in at Dinwiddie's factory in Bury during their formative years. Indeed, they might even have said it had proved the making of them.

Despite the passing of the Act, the problem still remained in knowing how far such measures were being carried out on the ground. With strong prompting from an MP by the name of Lord Ashley, the 1833 Factory Act had eventually been enacted with the avowed aim of ensuring that regulations were monitored and enforced. Incidentally, Lord Ashley was to play an important role in McDouall's life nine years later in 1842 on an occasion when the doctor would be asked to provide evidence to a Parliamentary Select Committee.

Under the terms of the 1833 Act, an Inspectorate of Factories had been created, responsible to the Home Office, with powers to impose penalties for infringements. However, in its early days, the number of recruits in post was to remain much too small in terms of the volume of officers required to cope with enforcing the terms of the Act in over 4,000 mills, predominantly in the north of the country.

The Poor Law Act of 1834 had been enacted by Government in order to reduce costs on an existing system which it believed was profligate in the amount of money spent on 'poor relief'. Its thinking was that 'handing out' money to poor people only further encouraged them in the habit of idleness. Instead, workhouses had been introduced with a system operating under which relief would only be given if a person committed themselves to the punishing regime of the institution. Conditions in these centres were so draconian as to deter any but the truly destitute from applying to go there. As was anticipated, even if financial savings were achieved, poverty itself became far more acute and widespread as a result of poor people feeling so desperate in trying to eke out some kind of subsistence living rather than having to 'end up in the workhouse'.

Returning to the Factory Act of 1833, it is interesting to note that, not long after McDouall had arrived in Ramsbottom two years later, it appears he made an effort to join the inspectorial ranks. However, evidence suggests he had not managed to progress very far with his application. It looked like he was unable to obtain a 'testimonial' from a certain local factory-owner.

∞

Back to McDouall's younger formative days, it is understood that at the time he had been carrying out his apprenticeship with the surgeon in Newton Stewart in the early 1830s, he had also shown an interest in political matters, taking part in debating societies in the nearby town of Castle Douglas and displaying early fluency as an orator. When gaining a place at the School of Medicine at Edinburgh University, he was pleased to see that the University also hosted debating societies which encouraged young trainees to participate in discussions centring around topical issues of the day.

By the time McDouall became a student in Edinburgh, widespread public interest had surfaced once again in what was happening in France. In July 1830, a 'second revolution' had occurred leading to the overthrow of the Bourbon monarch Charles X on the basis that he was ruling unjustly. Protesters in Paris had responded to repressive government measures by throwing up barricades and fighting with such force and conviction that it had caused Charles X to abdicate his throne. It might have seemed to observers abroad that, despite the monarch not being guillotined this time around, events much similar to 1789 were being re-enacted.

Keen as McDouall was to enter into the political debates of the time, he also though had to be conscientious in carrying out his medical studies at Edinburgh University. There is no direct account available from McDouall himself as to what his course of study there entailed, but it is possible to gain an idea from descriptions provided by a close contemporary of his by the name of Samuel Smiles.

Born in 1812, Smiles came from Haddington in the East Lothian area of Scotland and was studying medicine at Edinburgh University no more than a couple of years or so earlier than McDouall. From details Smiles recorded, it is interesting to learn what form a medical apprenticeship took at that time. In brief, Smiles outlined his training as mixing potions, bleeding and bandaging, and attending anatomy lessons. 'At the end of the course, following an oral examination of about an hour, I commenced my career as a doctor'.

Samuel Smiles was to become famous in later life, not as a doctor, but for writing a book entitled *Self-Help*, published in 1859, destined to sell a quarter of a million copies and earn the author fame not only in Victorian Britain but worldwide, particularly in America. Foregoing a career in medicine, Smiles would come to devote his energies to writing. In *Self-Help*, he was to argue that the progressive development of society ultimately depended not on collective action or on parliamentary legislation but on individuals adopting the practice of self-help. Interestingly, in this book which reads like a 'Who's Who' of Victorian Age entrepreneurs, the Grant Brothers were to gain a lengthy endorsement as examples of successful men who had become prosperous on the back of their own endeavours.

∞

At the time that Smiles and McDouall were undertaking their medical studies, Edinburgh University had established itself as a leading European centre of anatomical study with several teachers such as Alexander Monro, John Bell, John Goodsir and Robert Knox, all of whom are now regarded as having been pioneers in developing the subject of anatomy into a modern science. Knox in particular was a prominent practitioner. Qualifying as a doctor in 1814, the year McDouall was born, he had settled in Edinburgh in 1820 before becoming a Fellow of the Royal College of Surgeons in 1825. Whenever he lectured on anatomy, his lessons often took in 400 or more students at a time. These lessons concentrated on dissecting human corpses, a teaching methodology which was bound to impart a much more practical edge to medical training.

Smiles and McDouall, at the time they had embarked on their studies at Edinburgh University, could not help but have been aware of the controversies that had exploded into the public arena as to ethical considerations affecting the supply of human corpses for medical training purposes. Basically, practitioners such as Knox, given the increasing demand for cadavers, faced a shortfall in legal supply. This was not helped by Scottish law at the time which required that corpses used for medical research could only come from those who had died in prison, suicide victims or foundlings and orphans.

Illicit steps taken to offset this shortfall had eventually led to a police investigation uncovering a series of sixteen killings over a period of about ten months in 1828 carried out by William Burke and William Hare. It transpired they had been motivated to go on a murder spree on the basis they could earn the princely sum of between £8 and £10 for each corpse sold to Robert Knox for dissection at his anatomy lectures. As the principal instigator of this heinous practice, Burke had eventually been hanged on the morning of 28th January in front of a baying crowd of 25,000 onlookers. Ironically, his own corpse was publicly dissected by Professor Monro in the university's anatomy theatre.

What of the obvious suspicion of Knox's complicity in these murders? Cleared of this charge by a committee of inquiry, the feeling among his peers was nevertheless that he had been culpable in large measure for what had happened. He was to resign his post before eventually leaving Edinburgh in 1842 to embark on lecturing tours across Britain and mainland Europe.

∞

As for the 21-year-old young Peter Murray McDouall, at this point set to embark on a medical career of his own, it is clear to see how his outlook must have been shaped by formative experiences both in Newton Stewart and Edinburgh. Having obtained his diploma from the School of Medicine, McDouall would also have appreciated how important were the decisions lying ahead of him as to the exact direction in which he intended to pursue his future.

In basic terms, he could have settled for a safe position working in a quieter environment, perhaps in some relative backwater,

THE RADICAL UPBRINGING OF PETER MURRAY MCDOUALL

serving a largely upper/middle-class clientele. However, from what is known about his outlook to date, it is more probable the question nagged in his conscience: how could he contribute to the needs of a broader section of society?

With his inherent radical leanings, whichever location he happened to settle upon, he might have been seeking opportunity to offer his services for the benefit of less well-off members of society. Had he been looking to work in an environment where radical influence held sway, Lancashire would have had obvious appeal to him.

Why exactly Ramsbottom, it isn't clear. McDouall may have picked up something on the grapevine, encouraging him to believe that the Grant Brothers, fellow-Scots and reputedly philanthropic employers, might even offer up a template for how factory-owners should treat workers?

Irrespective of the thoughts that might have been occupying his mind before arriving in Ramsbottom in 1835, the experience that now lay ahead of him was destined, one way and another, to add further fuel to his radical outlook on life.

NOTES ON SOURCES

1. Given that there is no existing comprehensive biography of Peter
   Murray McDouall to draw upon - a good enough reason for
   writing this book in the first place - it has proved useful being
   able to tap into several available articles, written by different
   authors, relating to various stages or aspects of McDouall's life
   and times.

   Reference has already been made to the contributions made by
   writers, working under the banner of the Ramsbottom Heritage
   Society, providing a focus on McDouall's particular link with
   the town between 1835 and 1842. The following works have
   proved valuable by way of tracking episodes in McDouall's life
   from earliest times through to later years, including his broader
   involvement with Chartism from 1838 onwards:

   - *Friends of the People: Uneasy radicals in the age of the
     Chartists* a book which contains an article (pp.7-28)
     entitled *The People's Advocate*: Peter Murray McDouall
     (1814-1854) - written by Owen R. Ashton and Paul A.
     Pickering – published by The Merlin Press Ltd. (2002).
     As the authors say, this article draws a lot on the one
     cited below: *Pills, Pamphlets and Politics*.
   - *Peter Murray McDouall and Physical Force Chartism* an
     article (pp.53-84) in International Socialism (Spring
     1981 - Volume 12) written by Ray Challinor.
   - *Pills, Pamphlets and Politics: The Career of Peter Murray
     McDouall (1814-1854)* - an article (pp. 34-43) appearing
     in the Manchester Region Review (1997 – Volume XI)
     written by P. Pickering and S. Roberts.
   - Various items in the 'Chartist Ancestors' collection
     including two short pieces –*'Peter Murray McDouall,
     1814-1854'* and *'Portraits of Delegates No. 6: Peter McDouall.*

Peter Murray McDouall's contribution to the Chartist cause is also referred to in many other books addressing the history of the movement as a whole. Such sources will be noted at later stages with relevance to McDouall's involvement with Chartism from 1838 onwards.

2. Northern Star newspaper: 3 October 1840.

CHAPTER THREE

The Factory Town of Ramsbottom in 1835.

The Ramsbottom that Peter Murray McDouall came across in 1835 was naturally very different to the one that the Grant family had gazed down upon from their 'Top o' th' Hoof' vantage-point in 1783. A largely rural-looking landscape had been transformed in the meantime to one which now bore the indelible imprint of industrial development. Without question, the Grant family had been massively influential in the transitional process.

Winding the clock back to 1783 though, it is important to add that there was already quite a variety of industrial activity going on at that time and which had been taking shape over many decades previously. If William Grant senior had allowed his eye to wander beyond the River Irwell, he would have detected the outlines of such sites towards the far side of the valley in the area known as Carr Fold. The location of these work-places had been determined by proximity to fast-flowing hillside streams able to power water-wheels.

As far as trying accurately to recapture that view from the Bury Road, Hume Elliot's following description is likely to be very close to the mark: 'when thus surveyed for the first time by the Grants, Ramsbottom was little more than a place of farms and fields and orchards, rooks and trees, an ancient tannery and an old corn mill, with numerous streams of water flowing from unfailing springs far up the mountain side'. [1]

There was no recognisable town-centre at the time such as the one which was in process of development by the mid-1830s. It was the introduction of steam power that overwhelmingly changed the dynamics affecting location of industry. This in turn led to the growth of the 'Factory System' which, as far as business entrepreneurs were concerned, was far more cost and labour-intensive in producing goods. As a result, industry developed in new areas of the locality not needing to perch at the foot of a hillside.

When the first large mills were built, it was also imperative for factory-owners to provide sufficient housing nearby to accommodate their work-force. More often than not, recruitment involved bringing in workers from further afield, providing terrace-houses or humble cottages for them to move into. Built to modest specifications, no allowance seemed to have been made for the fact a worker might get married and go on to have a family. When this happened, as it did in most cases, it meant that these one-bedroom (or two if lucky) properties became hugely overcrowded. By their conditions of employment, workers were tied to such dwellings. Earning meagre wages, they could barely afford to pay existing rents, let alone think of moving to other more spacious properties there might be in the area.

The first big mill to be built, coincidentally starting up in the year 1783, had been when Bury-based business-partners, Robert Peel and William Yates, opened Ramsbottom Print Works for their expanding calico and bleaching business on a site to become known as 'The Old Ground'. Peel and Yates already had factories in Bury and at The Burrs. The influence Robert Peel had on the development of Ramsbottom, and indeed was to have on fostering the fortunes of the Grant family, cannot be underestimated. He was successful as a businessman to the extent that by 1800 he was one of only ten known millionaires in the country. He lived at Chamber Hall in Bury, where his even more famous son Robert (later to become Prime Minister) was born, the first of eleven children from his marriage in 1783 to partner's daughter Ellen Yates.

Not long after he had started up his operation in Ramsbottom, Robert Peel had become MP for Tamworth in the midlands in 1790.

A decade later, he had been created a Baronet, of Drayton Manor in the County of Stafford and of Bury in the County Palatine of Lancaster. By this time, having reached the age of 50, he was at the pinnacle of his business career. Becoming ambitious for his eldest son to reach even higher up the political ladder, he had furnished Robert with an expensive public school education and an entrée into the highest social circles. By the time he was eventually to die in 1830, most of his paternal ambitions had been achieved with son Robert by then not only having become an MP but occupying a Cabinet position as Home Secretary.

Going back to the time of building his factory in Ramsbottom, it had been a massive undertaking in 1783. Over time though, the site would develop obvious limitations. 'The Old Ground' still relied very much on water-power and was untidily spread out, a complex of workshops lying within the area bordered by Bolton Street, Bridge Street, Silver Street and Smithy Street.

Another major challenge facing Peel and Yates over time was to improve ways and means of transporting their textile products to the markets they were tapping into, both locally and beyond. This had led in 1799 to them funding the building of the Peel Bridge over the River Irwell and the construction of the Peel Brow stretch of roadway, providing a far more direct link to recently built roads such as the one connecting Bury and Haslingden with the Blackburn and Whalley turnpike road.[2]

∞

In 1802, the Ashtons, originally brothers James and John, had built Ramsbottom Mill, the town's first big spinning mill, located on Crow Lane. Writing in the 1870s, local author Benjamin Thomas Barton had commented that the spirit of political radicalism in Ramsbottom dated back to 1802 owing to this particular development. According to Barton, this stemmed from the fact the Ashtons had brought several skilled workers from their factory in Middleton to help make up the work-force in the newly constructed Ramsbottom Mill. Middleton, stated Barton, was 'one of the headquarters of the ultra-Radicals'. Samuel Bamford, born in 1788, historian, poet and radical agitator, was to become an influential figure who played an active part in organising the meeting in Manchester, which had ended in the infamous 1819 Peterloo Massacre.

Ramsbottom had sent a contingent of its own workers to that fateful gathering. Many amongst this number were to carry the scars with them for life; one man had died soon after from a flesh wound received in the arm. Meanwhile Bamford himself had been found guilty of 'inciting a riot' and sentenced to a year in Lincoln Prison. For all Bamford's revolutionary zeal, his experience in prison, together with the harrowing memory of what he witnessed that day in 1819, had left him disillusioned and convinced that state power would always succeed against radical militancy. He remained a voice for radical force but opposed to activism involving physical force.

∞

Another source of radicalism in Ramsbottom, according to Barton, and dating forward to the time of next-generation Ashton brothers, Samuel and Thomas, stemmed from the fact they had set up in 1831 the New Jerusalem Church of the Swedenborgians, built at the corner of Ramsbottom Lane and Factory Street. 'This sect, followers of the Swedish spiritual visionary Emanuel Swedenborg, was associated with holding unorthodox views on society. London artist and poet William Blake is probably the best known 'freethinker' to have been influenced by the movement who was to end up being charged in court in 1800 with uttering seditious words'. [3]

Samuel Ashton had already encouraged Swedenborgian ministers, much before 1831, to hold meetings on the third floor of their mill. He had also provided land nearby for the movement to build a chapel on the site of the New Jerusalem Church, becoming one of its first trustees. It may well have been that he supported the fundamental doctrines of this church. Perhaps more likely, he would have been prepared to give encouragement to any religious group that might help to have a civilising effect on the company's employees.

After all, this religious establishment was the only one currently in existence within the centre of town at that time. After the death of Samuel Ashton though, the age of the Swedenborgian influence, with its greater emphasis on free thinking, was becoming frowned upon by those in authority. The next generation of the Ashtons seemed intent on putting this particular religious connection behind them and instead donated land they owned for the purpose of building the town's first Anglican church, St. Paul's, in 1850.

As far as the Ashtons' continuing business operation in town was concerned, by the mid-1830s, Ramsbottom Mill was to have become the biggest mill in the Irwell Valley with three enormous waterwheels and three powerful steam engines. As in the case of Peel and Yates, the Ashtons too owned factories elsewhere in Lancashire, not only in Middleton but also Hyde. It is interesting to note that almost as soon as McDouall arrives in Ramsbottom, whereas he has few good things to say about the Grants, he is far more generous in his verdict on the Ashtons. It is more than likely that he would have found the record of greater tolerance shown by the Ashtons towards radicalism - at least as far as elder generations of the family had been concerned - much more conducive to his notion of how factory-owners should treat workers.

∞

It is clear though that the Ashtons were not seen as model employers in other of their business locations. For example, in Hyde, the Ashton family suffered tragedy with the assassination of one of their family, namely Thomas Ashton, aged 23 and eldest son of Samuel.

On 3 January 1831, Thomas had been shot dead at 7 o'clock in the evening, on his way home, by striking workers from Manchester who were lying in wait at the edge of the factory grounds. The ensuing investigation was to take until 1834 before the identities of the perpetrators of this crime were eventually to be uncovered: William Mosley, Joseph Mosley and James Garside. However, the co-accused were to provide conflicting evidence, each of them seeking to escape personal blame.

At the trial, James Garside, the one of the three whom judge and jury were finally to decide had fired the murderous pistol weapon, was held to have been asked by William Mosley: 'Which of the Ashtons did he think he had shot?'

The response William Mosley said he had been given was that: 'It didn't matter which it was, it was one of them'.

In the final analysis, judge and jury appeared to have been swayed by the testimony provided by William Mosley. Despite Garside having tried to switch the blame on to Joseph Mosley, and Joseph denying any knowledge of the crime, the two were held accountable between them for the murder of Thomas Ashton and sentenced to be hanged. Their executions took place on 25 November 1834 at Horsemonger Lane Gaol in London.

Although the broader cause of law and order might appear to have been vindicated by this judicial act of retribution, tension amongst workers remained at boiling-point throughout Lancashire from this point onwards, due to economic hardship and continued sense of grievance against factory-owners.

One curious aftermath to the murder of Thomas Ashton was that author Elizabeth Gaskell is believed to have based a literary work of hers on a very similar 'story-line'. In the novel, *Mary Barton*, she portrays the character Henry Carson, son of a wealthy mill-owner, being shot dead by the working-class Jem Wilson.

Coming back to McDouall though, despite the two towns being only 20 miles apart, it is unlikely he would have known much about

Hyde at the time he first started working in Ramsbottom in 1835. However, developing circumstances would bring him more directly in touch with what was going on there in future years.

∞

For their part, the Grants never seemed to miss a trick in fostering their own economic well-being. It helped greatly that their prospects were so actively promoted by Sir Robert Peel (father of the future Prime Minister). As Hume Elliot put it, 'Sir Robert Peel, by affording facilities (taking this to mean leasing out premises) 'proved helpful to them in their steady upward endeavours'. The biographer goes on to say: 'Sir Robert Peel found that these men, while cheerful, energetic, generous and good-natured, could always be relied upon'. Finally, 'after twenty-three years (since arriving in Lancashire in 1783) of hard toil, and enterprising and united industry…Messrs William Grant and Brothers purchased the print-works of Sir Robert Peel at Ramsbottom in 1806'. [4]

As to the nature of the property that the Grant Brothers acquired, Hume Elliot provides the following description: 'The print works, with valuable building land and the ample supply of water from the Holcombe Range, embraced about a dozen separate structures, some of which were of considerable magnitude, scattered about and, in some cases, lying right athwart the line of the principal streets of the present time, in the centre of the town of Ramsbottom'. [5]

From this point onwards, the rise of the firm of 'William Grant and Brothers' had proved meteoric. Hume Elliot comments that 'the cost incurred in buying The Old Ground had brought them under heavy financial responsibilities for years to come', but in the event it does not appear to have stood in the way of them taking on other large-scale business and personal property acquisitions through the 1810s and 20s.

In addition to the 1806 purchase, not long after in 1812 the Grants had gone on to buy Nuttall Mill, together with its surrounding estate, previously owned by a Mr Alsop. Incidentally, it was in relation to Nuttall Mill, and its attendant village cottage-dwellings, that McDouall was to carry out his investigative research into the effects of factory life, seeking subsequently to reveal his findings to a wider public audience.

Meanwhile, the decision the Grants were to take at the start of the 1820s - to re-locate from 'The Old Ground' to 'The Square' - proved not only the key to their own enhanced, future business prosperity but was also to bring about a whole re-shaping of the topography of Ramsbottom town by the mid-1830s. Moving their calico print business to 'The Square' (upon the site owned these days by the transport firm TNT), it opened up the vacated territory of 'The Old Ground' to a pattern of housing and commercial development that is still very much recognisable nearly 200 years later.

What were the factors prompting the Grants to make the move to 'The Square'? Apart from making a statement in terms of abandoning 18th century technology and adapting to modern-day steam-power, the new site offered a much stronger degree of security. In the manner of a castle, 'The Square' was surrounded on all sides in moat-like style by the River Irwell which, courtesy of its winding course, formed an imposing protective barrier.

Why the need for greater security? Crucially, it had to be taken into consideration that the climate of the time was one of increasing industrial tension and unrest. As far back as 1812, there had outbreaks of violence such as the so-called 'Luddite Riots', which, though taking place across a much wider area, also had strong local impact with workers threatening to break machines. [6]

As a site, 'The Old Ground' was open and exposed on all sides and would have been virtually impossible to defend against incursion by dissident elements intent on gaining entry and doing damage. What unfolded not long after at the nearby mill at Chatterton in 1826 was a sign of the vulnerability faced by all factory-owners at a time when new working practices were being introduced at ever faster pace.

Nor was what happened at Chatterton an isolated local incident. The installation of power looms in factories had become so prevalent, putting people out of work, that mobs of starving workpeople roamed round Lancashire looking to break into factories and destroy machines. In 1826, hardly a loom had been spared in Blackburn, Accrington, Darwen and Rossendale, and others in Wigan, Bolton and Clitheroe were saved only because the mills were heavily protected in the same way that The Square was in Ramsbottom.

On Wednesday, 26 April 1826, it had of course been William Grant, Justice of the Peace, who had borne the unenviable task of reading out the Riot Act at Chatterton. He recognised the seriousness of the problem facing all factory-owners from the risk of deteriorating industrial relations. Riding out on horseback, then in his late 50s, he would have seen himself faced with no alternative in the event but to issue the proclamation giving licence for soldiers to open fire on industrial workers. We do not have any written account regarding his reaction to taking this course of action that ended up in loss of lives. However much Grant would have regretted having to go to such lengths, he would still have seen it strictly within his duty to 'read out the Riot Act' in the best interests of maintaining law and order.

By way of further footnote, while no subsequent action was taken to address social and economic deprivations suffered by workers and their families, interestingly the Government elected to pay out full compensation to factory-owner, Aitken, for the damage done to his mill in April 1826.

∞

In his account of *The Story of The Cheeryble Grants*, Hume Elliot more often than not conferred priority on the parts played by the two brothers, William and Daniel, whom of course he steadfastly held up as the mirror-image of Dickens' Cheeryble Brothers.

There is no doubt that, between them, these two provided a powerful platform for the pursuit of the family's growing business interest. Hume Elliot remarks of William and Daniel, that though the latter was 'over twelve years his junior...each were the fitting complement of the other'. As the biographer goes on to explore the chemistry between them: 'One, William, had more of the 'microscopic element in his composition – could plod unwearyingly through the minute details of business'. Meanwhile, Daniel's 'mental mould was more telescopic'. Basically, William was seen as carrying out the anchor role in ensuring the business ran smoothly at ground level while Daniel was the one with the travelling brief to do everything to publicise the firm's products elsewhere in England but also abroad, for examples to locations as far distant as 'Batavia (Dutch East Indies), Singapore and Calcutta in the East and New Orleans, Baltimore and New York in the Western World'. [7]

Given that eldest Grant brother James had long since departed to Glasgow to start up a business of his own, what was Hume Elliot prepared to say about the impact made by the other brothers, John and Charles? Of John, it is stated that he had been 'more of a yeoman than a merchant or manufacturer' and had 'admirably managed the landed property acquired by the firm', namely the imposing Nuttall Hall. [8]

The Hall had about 20 rooms and a glazed dome in the roof. The large hall had combined chandeliers and fine tapestries. Portraits of parents William and Grace hung on the walls and it is said their sons seldom passed the pictures without an inclination of reverence or an exclamation of gratitude. The mansion was set in two acres of gardens, and also had extensive grounds and woodland walks with ponds and waterfalls.

Youngest brother Charles played a key role at a crucial time in the development of the family business. Born in 1788 in Lancashire, making him unique in the family in not being born in Scotland, Charles was to bear the distinction of being the best educated of the brothers, becoming an 'alumnus' of Bury Grammar School. Before this, the Grants had not come into contact much with what might be called formal education. After all, at an earlier point in time, it would have stood in the way of the practical need demanding the elder children work all hours to earn a wage to keep the family afloat.

As the Grant business grew, its management became more complex on different levels. Despite the undoubted strengths William and Daniel could offer in many ways, their attributes were more practical than strategic. Though much younger, it had been Charles who had seen the need to move away from 'The Old Ground' to a different site that would not only provide stronger security but also enable the Grants to concentrate their operation on a more compact scale.

Another aspect of security which the Grants would have been mindful of, particularly in view of the state-of-art technology they were installing within 'The Square', would have been the importance of cutting down on risks of industrial espionage at a time of fierce competition between manufacturers. It was Charles who took it upon himself to come up with a solution to the various issues facing the family-business at that time. Often, he had mounted his horse 'Wellington' at the crack of dawn taking him on long journeys to sites in bigger towns such as Hull and Nottingham where he had heard of developments unfolding that might offer a blueprint for a better way forward in Ramsbottom. Perhaps in this way, he had indulged in more than a bit of industrial espionage himself!

Eventually settling upon the site of 'The Square' – to be built three storeys high, with each of the four sides to be 80 yards long – Charles appointed John Cunliffe to be designer cum architect of the print-works. As far as construction was concerned, he engaged the services of Adam Brooks and other masons, whose work Charles superintended. The project had taken two years to complete - from 1820 to 1822 - with important landmarks along the way. As noted by Hume Elliot: 'the building was up at the first of its three storeys when the ox was roasted for the coronation celebration of George IV on July 19th 1821'. [9]

Much as the biographer was prone to dwelling on the memory of William and Daniel, it has to be said he was also fulsome in his praise for the part Charles played at this critical point in the further development of the Grant Brothers' business enterprise. For evidence of Charles' pivotal role, Hume Elliot based what he wrote on the testimony of one Elizabeth Wilson, who had served a good stint of time as maid at Grant Lodge. Surviving into her nineties, Elizabeth had provided much of the foregoing evidence, testifying to youngest brother Charles' contribution. Difficult as Hume Elliot might have found it, by way of deflecting praise away from the two wondrous 'Cheerybles', he trusted to the veracity of the detailed account passed on to him by Wilson.

For certain, it is known Charles lived close at hand in Ramsbottom during this critical period. Conveniently close to 'The Square', Barwood House had originally been built by another of Peel's partners, Henry Kay in the 1780s; it was subsequently acquired by John Rostron, a local industrialist, and was bought by Charles Grant in 1819. Alas, the youngest Grant brother was destined not to live there very long. In 1825, he died at the age of 37 from a seizure.

∞

While Charles had been the brother living in the heart of Ramsbottom, William and Daniel resided in style at 'Springside', a mansion they had bought in 1815, halfway between Bury and Ramsbottom. As a further indication of the wealth at their disposal, they had purchased Blackley Hall, near Manchester, with four acres of land adjacent. With unerring business sense, the two brothers looked to make themselves a profit by leasing out the premises for commercial purposes.

However, throughout the period that the Grants were developing the Ramsbottom side of their operation, William and Daniel still viewed their warehouse at no. 3 Cannon Street, in Manchester, as the hub of their business empire. It was the busy distribution centre of a widely-expanding operation.

As well as sharing residence with William at Springside, Daniel had also bought an elegant mansion on Mosley Street in Manchester in 1815. This was for them to have somewhere to live, near to the Cannon Street base, and also as a suitable place for William and Daniel to entertain the society of Manchester. It was used for such purposes until Daniel married Elizabeth Worthington later that year, when Mosley Street became their home.

While William himself never married, younger brothers Daniel and Charles had married sisters – daughters of Mr Worthington, resident of Sharson in Cheshire. Tragically, Daniel's marriage had only lasted a year before Elizabeth died at the age of 21 in 1816. There were no children from the marriage. Though her obituary appeared in the Manchester Mercury, the cause of her death was left unstated.

It was an even more testing time with William senior too passing away in 1817. Grieving after the loss of his young wife and father in quick succession, it is noted that Daniel's home on Mosley Street was later to return to what Hume Elliot described as 'a distinguished social rendezvous, always graced with the most generous hospitality... High jinks were not unknown in Mosley Street'. [10]

Diverting for a moment back to John Grant, as mentioned earlier, he seems to have much preferred playing out the role of the country squire at the grand Nuttall Hall which had been built to replace the quaintly-named Shipperbottom Farm on the Nuttall estate. The Grants in effect owned Nuttall village and John also had responsibilities for the working operation of the mill and hall farm. John, marrying Miss Jane Dalglish of Glasgow, appeared to have been the only Grant brother to bear children.

∞

However, certain records show that Daniel also fathered children. Evidence for this comes from the will he was later to draw up, in 1847, which included the following provisions:

'To my natural son, Daniel GRANT BRERETON, lately residing in South America but now of Manchester, the sum of five thousand pounds...I bequeath the following annuities, namely to my natural son Charles BRERETON an annuity of one hundred and fifty pounds during his life. To Elizabeth BRERETON the mother of the said Daniel GRANT BRERETON and Charles BRERETON an annuity of one hundred and fifty pounds during her life...' [11]

There is no record to say that Daniel and Elizabeth Brereton ever married. Their son Daniel Grant was born in Manchester sometime between May and June 1825. From about 1825 up until 1838, Elizabeth resided at Mosley Street and in 1829 she had given birth to second son Charles.

The domestic arrangement, not least with the children born out of wedlock, was a surprising one for Daniel to have entered into, particularly given the prevailing moral standards of the times. It is hard to think that Daniel's parents, both of course now deceased, would have easily countenanced their son's domestic arrangement with an unmarried woman. After all, William senior and Grace – dying in 1817 and 1821 respectively - had been puritanical in the way they had not only led their own lives but strongly steered their children in the same direction.

It is not known what exactly his brother William made of the situation but at the very least it must have been a severe embarrassment to him. It wouldn't have been possible to keep matters a total secret. Meanwhile, as far as others in Manchester reacted, Daniel appears to have incurred the disapproval of some of his business associates and contacts in social circles. It is not known what lengths Daniel and William may have gone to in trying to make sure employees, especially those in Ramsbottom, remained outside the loop. Perhaps it was fortunate for Daniel that the manner of his work was peripatetic by nature.

It was a detail in Daniel's life that Hume Elliot, writing long afterwards, discreetly chose to overlook. But then the overwhelming imperative for the biographer was to keep the reputation of the Grant family as pristine and unsullied as he could.

∞

Perhaps, with a sense of guilt about what their parents might make of things in their afterlife, it was no surprise that, from the late 1820s onwards, surviving members of the Grant family chose to focus to such a great extent on honouring the memory of father William and mother Grace. The remaining Grant children's self-evident desire to do everything possible they could by way of paying tribute to their beloved parents in subsequent years may also have contained an element of appeasement. After acquiring the Park Estate in 1827, the massively imposing Grants Tower was erected the year after. The Tower dominated the landscape in the same way that the Peel Monument (to be built in 1852) does in present times.

In addition to the factories, houses and memorial buildings that had served to change the appearance of Ramsbottom so much over a relatively short recent space of time, the Grant children, especially William, had been mindful of wanting to impart a spiritual element to the legacy of their parents. William was chiefly instrumental in the building of St. Andrew's Church – its construction taking place between 1832 and 1834 – keeping in mind the often-expressed wish of his father and mother to 'build a Sunday school and erect a church for the congregation with which the family were connected'.

This new church had been opened very recently on 15 June 1834.

It seemed as though the Grants regarded it as their mission to develop Ramsbottom as much as they could during these years. The Grants Arms was of course another property they were keen to expand in a more commercial sense, seeking to lease out the premises. This had not though proved such a successful enterprise at first. Over a short space of time, there had been three tenants in quick turnover. However, from 1st November 1834 onwards, George Goodrick, who had previously been on the staff of John Grant at Nuttall Hall, took on the job of landlord. Although Goodrick would continue in the role for the next fifty-five years thereafter, his tenancy was not to be without controversies, including most notably the one in which McDouall would present allegations to Parliament in 1842 in connection with payment procedures taking place at the Grants Arms contravening the terms of the Government's 1831 Truck Act.

∞

It was now more than ten years ago since the Grants had switched the site of their 'Old Ground' premises to 'The Square'. What impact had this had on the immediate area surrounding McDouall's newly-started medical practice at 18 Bolton Street?

The territory vacated, bordered by Bolton Street, Bridge Street, Silver Street and Smithy Street, from having been at first a desolate, abandoned piece of land, had now gradually started to become the heart of the 'new town' with a developing housing and commercial identity of its own. For a fair period of time, this area must have resembled a building-site but one which was to be rapidly transformed in character from the previous factory/ workshops environment that had dominated the neighbourhood. [12]

One of the first shops to come into being in this 'new town' was that opened about 1823 by grocer Henry Whittaker at 6 Bolton Street. Notable premises on the same street, virtually opposite where McDouall was to have his practice, were those at no. 23 opened around 1833 by John Hamer, local blacksmith, with his smithy, which occupied the cellar, giving the side-street its name. The 1842 Tithe Map shows terraced cottages having extended from the Market Place along each side of the turnpike Bolton road going through Ramsbottom between Bolton and Edenfield.

Bridge Street became built-up from the beginning of the 19th century onwards mostly with workers' houses which were later converted into shops. Some of the shops dated back to before the mid-1830s such as a confectioner's at no. 46. It is interesting to note that, whatever was still lacking in the way of shops at this time, there was no shortage of drinking establishments. The Rose and Crown, opened in 1797 on Carr Street and the first public house in Ramsbottom, had come into existence on the back of the opening of Peel and Yates' Old Ground factory. This pub had been built to save their workers, thirsting after hours spent bleaching and dyeing, having to face the strenuous ascent up the Rake to the only public houses then in the area, the White Hart and Shoulder of Mutton in Holcombe village.

As Ramsbottom went on developing though as an industrial town, the number of pubs increased significantly as well as the number of its beer houses. The distinction between pubs and beer houses was a curious one. The licensed premises of pubs and hotels 'were regulated by local magistrates, with wide-ranging powers to grant and revoke licences. They could sell spirits as well as beers and ciders and remain open throughout the night'. [13]

Meanwhile, so-called beer houses (with ale swigged down in pint pots at a proof value of 7%) had emerged in huge numbers in the aftermath of the 1830 Beer Act. In a rather short-sighted attempt to crack down on excessive cheap gin consumption, the government had made it possible at a single stroke for virtually anyone to have a licence granted to them for a small charge in order to open up shop between the hours of 5am and 10pm. The beer houses that proliferated from this time onward in Ramsbottom, as in other northern towns in the early 1830s, were often small premises, usually consisting of little more than the front room of someone's home.

It wouldn't take long for McDouall to pick up on the telling adverse effect that this factor, too, had on the health and well-being of a large section of the local population. In particular, that of factory-workers. Above all else, the young doctor would quickly detect there was little else for them to do in town but to drink their sorrows away during the limited time they were freed from the purgatory of slogging away at factory machines.

Notes on Sources

1. Hume Elliot, *The Country and Church of the Cheeryble Brothers* p. 71.

2. *Nuttall: Ramsbottom's Lost Village* – Ramsbottom Heritage Society (2020) provides a telling insight into the side-effects of the advent of the new turnpike road system, which served in time to isolate villages like Nuttall that had benefitted previously from being situated on the most commonly used trade-route operating in the area.

   Back in 1783, if the Grants had taken it upon themselves to travel down to Ramsbottom from the direction of the old Bury road, they would have found their route much more circuitous than the one nowadays descending directly down Peel Brow or Bury New Road. A journey, at that earlier time, would instead have involved negotiating a back-route starting out from the top of the hill at Shuttleworth, traversing down Shipperbottom Lane (a route finally to be cut off completely by the M66!), then Nuttall Road and Nuttall Lane before reaching a junction linking up with the road leading from Holcombe Brook towards Ramsbottom.

   The building of the Peel Bridge in 1799 was to prove a massive breakthrough in improving trading links between Peel and Yates' factory and retail outlets lying beyond. Incidentally, the route across Peel Bridge was open for other road-users. However, in the nature of the times, Peel and Yates were not so philanthropic as to provide this service free. A toll-house stood – on the site of what is now the Wharf riverside picnic area – which levied sums from other road-users. Despite its unpopularity, this lucrative practice was to remain in force until the year 1900.

   Peel Brow had been built also for the purpose of connecting Ramsbottom up with the turnpike road between Bury and Blackburn. Increased economic demand, prompting the need for improved road transport, had undoubtedly played a key part in transforming both the system and standard of road-building at this time. Authorised by Parliament, with powers granted to collect road tolls in order to build and maintain principal highways, turnpike trusts operated not only within Lancashire but across the country as a whole.

3. Andrew Todd's article *Radical Ramsbottom* (RHS News Magazine no. 32: Summer edition 2007) provides a fascinating account of radical activity in Ramsbottom in times pre-dating McDouall. The article also drew the author's attention in the direction of the 19th century historian, Benjamin Thomas Barton. Barton wrote the *History of the Borough of Bury and Neighbourhood in the County of Lancaster* (1874), in which he makes specific mention of Ramsbottom pp. 208-212.

4. Hume Elliot, *Church and Country of the Cheeryble Brothers* p. 72.

5. Hume Elliot, *The Story of the Cheeryble Grants* p. 118.

6. The word 'Luddite' has of course come to have wider connotations since first coined back at the start of the 19th century. Historically speaking, the term was associated with bands of workers intent on destroying machinery, especially in cotton and woollen mills in the early 1810s, the use of which they held to be unfairly threatening their jobs. In a rather more derogatory-sounding sense though, the term has come to be applied to anyone perceived as old-fashioned in their unwillingness to adapt to new technology. Returning to the historical sense, the 'legend' appears to have grown up around a character by the name of Edward Ludlam (shortened to Ned Ludd) who in 1799 smashed up textile machines in Nottinghamshire as a means of commending the honest toil of workers as opposed to slavish dependence on machinery.

7. Hume Elliot, *The Story of the Cheeryble Grants* pp. 121-3.

8. Ibid p. 121.

9. Ibid p. 132.

10. Ibid p. 120.

11. Alan Hitch's article *Daniel Grant, famous or infamous?* (RHS News Magazine no. 30: Spring edition 2006) pulls no punches in exposing the 'double life' of Daniel Grant. Incidentally, this article is distilled from a longer piece of unpublished work he wrote - *Daniel Grant: a character study of a Manchester merchant* – which is stored at Bury Library/Archives.

12. *Ramsbottom's Heritage: Industrial Village, New Town and Railway 1783-1846*, a video created in 2006 by the RHS, provides a stimulating visual representation as to how the centre of Ramsbottom, as we know it today, came into being during the course of those formative years.

   Another visual source, the *Archive Photographs Series: Around Ramsbottom* – compiled by Andrew Todd and the RHS (Chalford Publishing Company, 1995) provides striking pictorial evidence of local people and places in past times.

13. An excellent exhibition was mounted in 2018 by the RHS at the Heritage Gallery, Ramsbottom Library, bearing the resonant title (courtesy of King James I's legislative act of 1606) of *Ramsbottom Pubs & the Odious and Loathsome Sin of Drunkenness*. The quoted passage in the text is taken from the booklet accompanying the event bearing the same title - p. 2.

CHAPTER FOUR

McDouall Takes on the Grants
and Ends Up a Chartist.

Given his medical background, McDouall was naturally well-qualified to diagnose causes and symptoms of ill-health. He saw it that factory workers were trapped within a system that put them at constant risk of physical breakdown and injury. Having experienced something similar back in Newton Stewart, he reckoned though that what he encountered in Ramsbottom was on a far worse scale.

McDouall could of course command fees for his services, but from the start he did so only for those patients who were well-off financially. Knowing that factory workers would always struggle to afford the money, it was not in his character to stand back and watch them suffer. Very soon after arriving in Ramsbottom, he was attending such patients freely and doing whatever else to lend support.

It is clear that he took steps to approach employers to argue the rights of workers to have better working and living conditions. However, adding insult to injury from finding his pleas ignored, patients soon were letting it be known they had come under instruction from employers not to visit him. Soon after this, he found he was prevented from attending cases or accidents that occurred within factories. Not that any outright ban was imposed. In simple terms, he just was never called. Again, inquiries as to whys and wherefores were glossed over. Much as he might have welcomed an opportunity, the chance never fell to him to visit the factories to examine conditions first hand. He realised he would have to work out alternative steps to address the problems he was witnessing all around him.

It appears, as referred to earlier, that at one point he became interested in applying to become a member of the factory inspectorate established under the terms of the 1833 Factory Act. To do so though entailed obtaining a testimonial from a person of standing in the community. Although not mentioning McDouall directly by name, Hume Elliot describes an interesting episode when a medical practitioner of the place asked Daniel Grant one day to sign a testimonial, with a view to securing an appointment as a factory inspector.

'No! No!' Daniel is reported to have said to the request, 'I sign none of these things!' However, it is said by the Grants' biographer that Daniel 'had the kindliest feelings towards the young doctor'. He is portrayed as wanting to lend any help he could, barring that of providing a testimonial. 'Ask me for £500 if you want it, but I can't put my hand to anything of that sort'.

The reference to 'the young doctor', without mentioning a specific name, may be held to provide something of a clue to possible identity. Hume Elliot explains Daniel's reluctance by pointing out it was a common trait among the Grant family never to write anything down on paper if they could help it. He goes on to say that 'one requires to remember that the education of these elder brothers had been very imperfect and that an early experience of trouble and annoyance, arising from putting their hand to a document, in all probability gave rise to this lifelong aversion'. [1]

In whatever way Hume Elliot chooses to explain Daniel's reluctance to provide a reference for the 'young doctor', McDouall was never in the event to become a factory inspector.

∞

Another route that McDouall took to try and highlight the adverse effects of the factory system was by undertaking a detailed survey of workers' living conditions in the Ramsbottom area. To this end, he visited over 300 cottages occupied by factory labourers and their families in order to collect information. The emerging evidence provided a damning indictment of the way workers were being treated.

Later, on 24 August 1838, he was to present his research findings to a meeting of the British Association at Newcastle-upon-Tyne. In January 1839, a paper was published, providing details of worker exploitation. Quoting from this paper, it is evident McDouall included a wide range of cottages - 309 in total - in his survey, concentrating on three main areas of research which he saw as affecting people's lives adversely: overcrowding, wage levels and educational prowess.[2]

With regard to overcrowding, statistics showed a total of 2,000 individuals occupying the 309 cottages surveyed, 137 of which had one bedroom and the remaining 172 having two bedrooms. Overall, it meant that there was an average of 6.47 per abode. Breaking this figure down to cottages having either one or two bedrooms, the ratios worked out at an average of 5.16 members in one-bedroom and 7.11 in two-bedroom properties. High as the average figures showed, there were many instances at the top end of each category, either one or two-bedroom, that revealed overcrowding on a horrendous scale, with 42 households having occupancy-rates reaching double figures per dwelling.

Out of the 2,000 residing in these 309 properties, 1,134 were in receipt of wages. Although the wage-levels were generally as low as might have been expected, and especially in terms of what could be afforded in the way of putting food on the family table, one or two interesting divergences arose in McDouall's findings. In particular, he discovered that workers employed at the Ashton Brothers' factory received much higher wages than those carrying out comparable jobs at the Grants' factories.

In educational terms, McDouall found that the number of 'persons' out of the 2,000 'who could read was 1,319 or 66 per cent of the whole number' while the corresponding figure for writing was '531 or 26.5 per cent'. He added that 'few of these persons could read or write well – the majority are learners'.

If McDouall was hoping that his audience at the August meeting in Newcastle-upon-Tyne might take serious note of his findings, he was to be disappointed. Ironically, the main follow-up from the British Association was to congratulate the Ashtons for the fact that they paid their employees comparatively better wages than the Grants did. Although the paper does not state details specifically, it is thought that the majority of the cottages represented in the survey must have included the village of Nuttall, where people working in the Grant-owned Nuttall Mill lived. Even so, the census for 1841 was to show only 124 cottages in Nuttall. The additional 185 homes surveyed by McDouall would have come from other areas of Ramsbottom, for example on Crow Lane, close to the Ashtons' mill.

In a short space of time since arriving in 1835, McDouall had made no bones about showing his opposition to the factory system and broadcasting his concerns publicly. Having gone to the trouble of carrying out his research though, he had little to show in the way of progress at the end of the process. None of this however was to act as a deterrent to McDouall in the future. From 1838 onwards, he became even more determined, only deciding on other means to demonstrate the extent to which he held that workers were treated callously by employers such as the Grant Brothers.

∞

Returning for a moment though to the paper he delivered to the British Association, McDouall undertook his survey at a time when this type of statistical method was by no means fully established as a tool of social investigation. Apart from this, it was likely he took his research findings to the wrong forum for the type of response he had been seeking. In truth, the British Association placed more store by trying to improve scientific methodology rather than for example getting involved with studies relating to people's working and living conditions.

Without any doubt though, McDouall was ahead of his time in what he had attempted to do to highlight the need to take steps to combat poverty. By the start of the 1840s, authority attitudes would begin to change after a civil servant called Edwin Chadwick was asked by parliament to investigate living conditions in Britain that culminated in his 1842 *Report on the Sanitary Conditions of the Labouring Population*. Statistics in the report showed just how unhealthy industrial towns were. Chadwick's findings were to cause something of a shock when he concluded that much poverty and ill-health was caused by terrible living conditions and not for example, as conveniently argued up to this point by hard-liners, by innate working class idleness.

Health matters came to be taken more seriously after the passing of the Public Health Act in 1848 with a Board of Health being set up to take measures to improve living conditions and standards of sanitation in towns across the country. Local authorities were empowered to appoint a health officer, who incidentally had to be a legally qualified medical practitioner. It was a role that would ultimately have suited McDouall even if it wasn't until a decade later that such opportunities were to arise.

∞

For the time being, in these early years practising medicine in Ramsbottom, McDouall's pioneering efforts to lay bare the levels of poverty in places such as Nuttall were still failing to achieve the impact he had hoped for. Incidentally, it was at this same time in 1838/9 that Dickens' novel *Nicholas Nickleby*, with its attributed characterisation of William and Daniel as the philanthropic Cheeryble brothers, was being serialised in magazine-form across the country. The findings of McDouall's research by contrast, although having nothing like a comparable readership, provided material though that the Grants would have been far less happy about and made strenuous efforts to defend themselves against.

Hume Elliot quotes in its entirety a letter written by William Grant, dated May 17 1839, for the benefit of a certain 'London correspondent'. This said 'correspondent' was apparently in process of compiling a piece of work which 'aimed at depicting in their true light the truly benevolent, patriotic, and energetic exertions of such individuals as the Grants, to whom the country at large, and Lancashire in particular, is so much indebted'.

In the midst of William's three-page letter in response - a worthy enough accomplishment in its own right for someone who the biographer had given to believe was, in common with Daniel, ever reluctant to put pen to paper - there is an extended section following on from the simple opening statement: 'In 1812 we purchased Nuttall factory...'

What follows on from this is a lengthy justification, almost self-asserted eulogising, itemising the whole host of measures the Grants had taken to turn Nuttall into what seems a veritable paradise for workers:

'In consequence of the death of Mr Alsop, the workpeople had been long short of employment, and were very destitute. We ordered the manager to get new machinery of the first-rate construction, and greatly extended the building; and before we began to spin or manufacture we clothed the whole of the hands at our expense, prepared an entertainment for them, and observed that the interests of masters and servants are bound together, that there are reciprocal duties to perform, that no general or admiral could be brave unless he was supported by his men, that we knew how to reward merit, and would give constant employment and liberal wages to all our faithful servants; and I am happy to say that they, as well as those at our printing establishment, with very few exceptions, have conducted themselves with great propriety'. [3]

The content of William's letter serves to show how the Grants were always intent on portraying their entrepreneurial role in a wholly positive light. Certain phrases appear very telling to the modern ear in terms of nuance, for example 'masters and servants' but then few people living at the time would have seen reason on that account to take offence. Much as reading this section of the letter would have made McDouall's teeth grind, frustratingly he wouldn't have needed reminding that this was what he was always up against in attempting to highlight the true conditions workers had to endure.

∞

What else could McDouall do to expose the situation faced by workers? Beginning to feel something of a lone voice in the wilderness, McDouall had been heartened at this time through coming into contact with a fellow doctor from Bury by the name of Matthew Fletcher. Nearly twenty years McDouall's senior, Fletcher was to have a strong influence on his younger colleague, eventually steering him towards the fledgling movement of Chartism.

A great grandson of John Kay, inventor of the Flying Shuttle, Fletcher had studied medicine at St. Bart's in London and qualified as a member of the Royal College of Surgeons in 1818. By 1821, he was a practising surgeon, living at 59, Union Square, in Bury. An outspoken critic himself of the abuses of the factory system, Fletcher already knew what it was like to be stigmatised as a radical. After all, within the social circles he had been used to moving in previously, it was said that radicalism was considered a more serious moral stain on the character than a charge, say, of financial dishonesty would have been. Fletcher had nailed his colours to the Chartist mast having become an elected delegate for the Bury district, which incorporated Ramsbottom as an outlying area.

Keeping up with the politics of the day, it was probable McDouall would have already been aware of the birth of Chartism during the last year or two. What he grasped from Fletcher was the potential impact the movement might have for him personally in terms of his ambitions to campaign on behalf of the working class.

∞

Chartism had originated as a movement in 1836 when a group of workers in London had founded the 'London Working Men's Association'. One of its members, William Lovett, had been responsible for a publication entitled *The People's Charter* as recently as May 1838. The movement was to gain its current name from the fact the document put forward six basic political objectives for the government to consider and act upon. Each of these objectives sought to address what were seen as impediments militating against the proper entitlement of the working classes to have a justifiable say in how the country was run.

The 'six points' for political reform were summarised in terms of demands for:

- Universal manhood suffrage
- Equal electoral districts
- Vote by secret ballot
- Annual elected parliament
- Payment of members of parliament
- Abolition of property qualifications for membership

Taking each of these 'six points' in turn, the first one was the most central in terms of demanding the right for every man to be able to vote. This was no doubt a response to the perceived shortcomings of the 1832 Reform Act which had enfranchised the middle class but left the working class out on a limb. On a parallel note, although many women were to play an active role in the movement, it was always later to be a cause for regret that Chartism had omitted the voting rights of women from consideration.

Secondly, the question of differing sizes of constituencies had continued to vex Chartists. Even though the 1832 Act had removed so-called 'rotten boroughs', where often a singular number of registered voters enjoyed the power of voting in an M.P. of their own, huge inconsistencies still remained. It was held that this issue could only properly be addressed through creating 'equal electoral districts' in terms of levelling voter numbers across constituencies.

Thirdly, the practice of secret ballot was seen as important to introduce, in the light of all the pressures that were exerted on voters at the time at public hustings, including threats and bribery. Fourthly, as impractical as annual elections might have sounded on a logistical basis, the idea here was to keep the workings of parliament more continuously open to scrutiny. Fifthly, the demand that MPs should be paid stemmed from the fact that currently only people with sufficient existing money behind them could afford to take up an unpaid role.

Lastly, the existing regulation that prospective MPs had to meet stringent property qualifications was seen as unfair and prohibitive to the vast number of people in the country unable to satisfy such restrictive criteria.

∞

In essence, there was nothing new or original in what was contained in the People's Charter. These ideas had been in circulation since the 1770s. The difference now was in presentation of the 'six points' in a way which was cohesive, snappy and much more eye-catching. Besides this, the choice of the word 'charter' provided a rallying-cry for bringing people together under one banner: to finish off the work that the other great charter – Magna Carta – had begun. Unquestionably, the notion succeeded in capturing the popular imagination in the late 1830s. [4]

However, not everyone who was to subscribe to the cause of Chartism was bound to see things in purely historical or political terms. In fact, the Chartist movement was destined to take shape as more of an umbrella movement, fusing together a host of groups and causes. Although many of these were inter-related, it meant that different people joined up for different reasons. For example, while widespread resentment was still felt at the shortcomings of the 1832 Reform Act, others signed up to the cause more by way of resentment with the factory system and/or the Poor Law Amendment Act of 1834.

∞

Returning though to the discussions taking place between Fletcher and McDouall, the more experienced of the two doctors impressed upon his younger colleague all the concerns he too had felt in the face of trying to counter the effects of the factory system. McDouall would have found it comforting to learn that Fletcher had trodden a similar path before subscribing to Chartism. The idea of signing up to membership of this large, national-based movement, with its system of local representation, would no doubt have had strong appeal for McDouall, coming as it did on the endorsement of a respected professional colleague such as Fletcher.

To give him a chance to see for himself, Fletcher had invited McDouall to attend a meeting in Bury in October 1838, and asking him to say a few words by way of introduction to the assembled throng. While the young doctor was said to have made something of a name for himself in a debating society back in Castle Douglas, he appears to have given a stuttering performance at this meeting. Fellow Chartist, Gammage, was later to record that those hearing the young doctor speak on that occasion must have held 'little hope of his success in that department'. [5]

In his defence, it is likely McDouall must have found himself somewhat 'put on the spot', or perhaps been nervous on the occasion finding himself in unfamiliar company. On all subsequent occasions he spoke, it is evident he was rated a most effective orator.

Aware that the movement was looking to bring in promising new recruits, particularly if they might have leadership potential, Fletcher would certainly have seen McDouall as a man in his own mould, idealistic and able to command the respect of followers. Indeed, an opportunity for the younger man to play a prominent role in the movement was to come amazingly quickly and in highly unusual circumstances - following the dramatic arrest of the Chartist delegate for Ashton-under-Lyne - the Rev. Joseph Rayner Stephens, on 27 December 1838.

∞

At that point in time, the Rev. Joseph Rayner Stephens was probably the most renowned spokesperson for the cause of Chartism across the whole of the country. Born in Edinburgh in 1805, he had moved to Manchester when his minister father was posted there in 1819. He attended Manchester Grammar School. Serving as a teacher for two years, he then trained to become a preacher. In 1829, he had been ordained and appointed minister of the Wesleyan Church in Cheltenham but in 1834 had been expelled from this post for expressing political views that were seen to be not consistent with his role as a minister.

Moving soon after to Ashton-under-Lyne, he had found it a much more conducive setting in which to project his views. He had been able to set up his own brand of 'Stephensite' churches in Ashton and nearby Stalybridge. From the pulpit, he railed against the injustices perpetrated by mill-owners on their workers and was particularly critical of the Government's Poor Law Act of 1834 which, he argued strenuously, put added shame and pressure on poor people in return for any form of aid the state lent them.

For sure, such messages were much better received in Ashton than in Cheltenham! In this new setting, Stephens quickly made a name for himself as an exponent of views showing strong empathy with the plight of the working man, trapped within a web of neglect and poverty. It was natural that he should be invited to speak at Chartist meetings which embraced such issues. Even if he wasn't quite prepared to sign up formally to the political objectives of the movement, he still very much saw himself as a fellow-traveller seeking ways of addressing the social and economic problems faced by the working class at this time.

Not that the Government of the day was prepared to make any concession to Stephens. Irrespective of whether he purported to be Chartist or not, his influence was regarded as highly dangerous. With his powers of rhetoric as a public speaker, he was seen as having massive potential to whip up impressionable crowds of listeners to engage in unlawful, rebellious activity.

∞

A decision taken at the end of December 1838 to arrest Stephens revealed a lot about the Government's response at the time to the sudden, new threat that the Chartist movement posed across the north of England and in particular certain 'hot-spots' in Lancashire.

Throughout 1838, the Government had found it very difficult keeping track of Chartism and the pace at which it was gaining in popularity with workers. It was no longer a question of having to deal with sporadic bouts of localised agitation, more an orchestrated national campaign that was proving successful in attracting thousands of people at a time to attend meetings taking place at selected public venues across the country. Particular speakers seemed to have been singled out for their effectiveness in spelling out the need to take action to address injustices in how the country was being run. For all his protestations of not being a fully-signed up Chartist, Stephens was undoubtedly at the top of lists of speakers invited to express their views and opinions at such events.

Kersal Moor in Salford had been the scene of perhaps the most spectacular Chartist meeting held that year, occurring on

Monday 25 September 1838. The Moor was a large open space which attracted large congregations of people attending all kinds of events. Since the late 1700s, it was noted for its horse-racing course as well as one or two strange-sounding other spectacles that had gone on from the 18th century onwards. One of these for example was 'races' involving nude males, apparently designed to allow females to 'study form' before choosing mates. Stakes could apparently be high on such occasions. Indeed, in 1796, one Roger Aytoun, known locally as 'Spanking Roger', later to become a national hero after the lengthy siege of Gibraltar that had preserved the island from Spanish take-over, reaped the jackpot of acquiring Hough Hall in Moston through marriage to the widowed Barbara Minshull (then aged 65 and twice her suitor's age) following her admiring attendance at one such event at which he had displayed his sporting wares to striking effect.

Be that as it may, fast forward to 1838...and a huge crowd, estimated at 300,000, had assembled on Kersal Moor early in the day. According to eye-witness Gammage, this monumental gathering represented workers from many miles around, whose 'haggard emaciated features bore evidence of suffering'. Joseph Rayner Stephens, with his reputation as a fiery radical parson from Ashton, had been invited as one of the speakers at the event. It is certain he not only made a name for himself with his audience on that day, but at the same time also managed to make an indelible mark on a Government that was already much beset about the course of events unravelling in parts of the country such as Lancashire.

The tenor of what Stephens put forward on the day held true to his strong belief that the day-to-day life of the working-class man was, as things stood, being delivered a disservice which the government needed to redress. In essence, he stated that if any man asked him what he meant by universal suffrage, he would tell him that 'every working man in the land had a right to a good coat on his back, a good hat on his head, a good roof for the shelter of his household, a good dinner upon his table, no more work than would keep him in health whilst at it, and as much wages as would keep him in plenty, and in all the enjoyments of all the pleasures of life which a reasonable man could enjoy'. [6]

For Stephens, as he emphasised during the course of his presentation at Kersal Moor, everything boiled down to the Chartist campaign being viewed as a 'knife and fork' issue which could best be determined by taking measures to feed mouths. Reasonable-sounding as this argument might have appeared to many, the authorities took a different view, becoming determined one way or another to gag the reverend gentleman.

∞

The powers that the Government had to police such situations were however few. The London Metropolitan Police service itself, through the offices of the younger Robert Peel, then Home Secretary (leading to recruits being called 'peelers' or 'bobbies') had only been formed as recently as 1829. Elsewhere in the country, any police presence on the ground was very patchy.

It is worthwhile to note the comments of Sir Charles Napier, who was in charge of the Government's armed forces in the North at this time. He had ridden to Kersal Moor in September 1838 and concluded that 'the Government should be prepared to consider the Charter in Parliament. There is no wisdom in letting complaints be rejected and pikes made'. It appears Napier made efforts to keep violence to a minimum and calm tensions in the area as best he could whilst still obeying his orders. Napier blamed 'Tory injustice and Whig imbecility' for the conflicts, and privately pitied the Chartists rather than feared them'. [7]

Naturally, the Government took a different view and wouldn't have allowed its policies to be based on anything approaching military expediency. In order to take more effective action against the situation of widespread national unrest facing the Government in 1838, new tactics were devised, aimed at tackling a problem that was threatening to get out of hand.

In December 1838, illustrating the need to resort to whatever means available, the Bow Street Runner Henry Goddard (belonging to an early form of police force attached to Bow Street Magistrates Office in London) had been dispatched north to keep an eye out on Chartist torchlight meetings taking place in Leigh, Bury and Todmorden. However it was to be the meeting he attended in Ashton-under-Lyne on 27 December that was to have most telling impact on the turn of events.

As Goddard was later to write in his memoirs, in addition to keeping 'an eye out', he had further been called upon to carry out the high-risk strategy of taking it upon himself to arrest Stephens. The disconcerting aspect of this, as he was later to recount, had been 'how it was to be executed without the sacrifice of human life'. Above all else, he wrote, 'it required great caution, as there were some thousands of spinners who would rise to a man and come forward to resist his lawful apprehension. Under the circumstances it would not be considered safe to attempt it without the aid of Military power, inasmuch as Stephens was so idolized and worship'd by all the operatives that there was not a family in all Ashton and other places but had got his portrait manufactured on all their tea cups, plates and saucers, he was held in such high esteem among them'.

Notwithstanding all this, Goddard had managed to effect an arrest which appeared by the Bow Street Runner's account of events, to have taken place in very fortuitous circumstances when he and a colleague happened to catch sight of Stephens out walking alone in daylight hours in Ashton. Following him, they observed him enter the premises of the Bush Inn. At a time when it was far from busy, they promptly took the opportunity to arrest and remove him without further ado. Goddard subsequently handed Stephens over to New Bailey Prison, Manchester, where he was held for further examination, 'which occupied the two following days. then he was again remanded until the 3rd of January, and after a lengthy examination was committed for trial or to find bail himself in £1,000 and two sureties of £500 each'. [8]

Although released on bail after his arrest in December 1838, Stephens concluded he was not well-placed to go on serving as delegate for Ashton-under-Lyne. It must have considerably added to his worries knowing he had a court case ahead of him. Taking stock of who could take over the role, with the young doctor from Ramsbottom having made a favourable impression during the course of two or three meetings, following an introduction from Fletcher, Stephens had recommended McDouall as his successor to Ashton constituents.

A meeting had then been hastily convened, chaired by William Aitken, a local schoolmaster who was thereafter to become a great friend and supporter. McDouall was duly elected to serve as Ashton's Chartist district representative from the start of 1839 onwards.

∞

Despite having to operate in another location unfamiliar to him, McDouall was out to do his very best by his new constituents. With help from the likes of Aitken, he adapted to the new role as quickly as he could. A town just outside Manchester, fifteen miles from Ramsbottom, Ashton possessed some of the largest factories in the country, together with the most modern machinery. Rapid economic expansion had led to an equally rapid influx of labour and it had become 'perhaps the most radical and Chartist of all the factory towns'. [9]

Essentially a working class stronghold, Ashton had grown from a one-time small market town at the start of the century to a cotton centre which would have a population of 45,235 by the time of the 1841 census. Many times the size of population of Ramsbottom, the prospect of serving as a delegate to Ashton posed a huge challenge for McDouall to take on but one he was keen to take on.

The town's population largely consisted of young men, including a large influx of Irishmen, who, for the benefit of picking up a wage in hard times, had resigned themselves resentfully to the harsh industrial discipline imposed on them. Not altogether unfamiliar with this type of situation from his experience in Ramsbottom, the main difference was that Chartism in Ashton had the backing of a far stronger contingent of activists. [10]

McDouall could not have failed to pick up on the degree to which his new constituents craved for militant tactics to be used to retaliate against heavy-handed measures that were being taken by the Government, such as the arrest of Stephens.

∞

This new role, much as it came as a bolt from the blue, had not only the effect of propelling McDouall into the spotlight but also presenting him with a wonderful opportunity to deliver on the programme he had set for himself of championing the cause of working people. Overcoming the disappointment he had experienced after Newcastle, he could now see a much more direct way to channel his ambitions by way of acting as Chartist delegate for Ashton-under-Lyne.

For McDouall, whilst this new development was bound to impose an obvious question-mark on the level of his existing commitment to Ramsbottom, medical or in other capacity, he was still determined to maintain a high profile there. Despite the time he spent in Ashton, he maintained his residence at 18, Bolton Street. Tithe survey details reveal that this was where he went on living up to 1842. For certain, McDouall was to go on being strongly involved in what was happening in Ramsbottom. Nor was he about to let up on his investigations into questionable practices being carried out by the Grants.

It is fair to say though that McDouall's existence took on a new lease of life at the start of 1839, both on the back of his commitment to Chartism and then his sudden appointment to the post of delegate for Ashton. His horizons were undoubtedly expanding from this time onwards.

Notes on Sources

1. Hume Elliot, *The Story of the Cheeryble Grants*, pp. 155-6.
2. Details of McDouall's presentation at Newcastle are taken from a paper *Statistics of the Parish of Ramsbottom, Near Bury, in Lancashire* by PM McDouall, published in the Journal of the Statistical Society of London, Vol. 1, No. 9 (Jan., 1839), pp. 537-539.
3. Hume Elliot, *The Country and Church of the Cheeryble Brothers*, pp. 94-6.
4. The point made about no 'new' substance being put forward in *The People's Charter* is one expressed by Malcolm Chase, *Chartism: A New History* (2007). Other texts, on the broader issue of the history of Chartism that will be referred to in the course of this narrative, in addition to the previously-mentioned one by Gammage, are:
   - *Memoirs of a Social Atom* by WE Adams – published in 1903. Adams (1832-1906) was a Chartist, republican, supporter of women's suffrage, and served 36 years as Editor of the Newcastle Weekly Chronicle. After retiring from the post, he wrote his memoirs based on having met several, notable Chartists in his teens and twenties, including McDouall.
   - *The Chartist Movement* by Mark Hovell (Manchester 1918). Hovell (1888-1916) wrote one of the first histories about Chartism as an author who was not a first-hand witness to events. A distinctive aspect of this biography though is that, whilst serving in World War One, Hovell was killed in action. The book he had been writing was in the end completed by another hand, that of Thomas Tout.
   - *The Making of the English Working Class* by EP Thompson (Harmondsworth 1980).
   - *The Chartists* by Dorothy Thompson (Temple Smith: London 1984).

While many other general histories on Chartism have been included in the research, it is felt that Gammage, Adams and Hovell have the most distinctive, substantial statements to make regarding McDouall's specific input.

5. Gammage, *History*, p 67.
6. Edmund and Ruth Frow, *Radical Salford: Episodes in Labour History* (Neil Richardson 1984) p. 11.
7. Sir W. Napier, *The Life and Opinions of General Charles James Napier* (1857 Vol. 2) p. 39.
8. Henry Goddard, *Memoirs of a Bow Street Runner*. Relevant section contained in *Arrest of the Revd. R. Stephens, Chartist & Torchlight Agitator* – pp. 154-161. N.B. The arrest of Stephens was one of the last actions carried out by the Bow Street Runners, before the organisation was merged into the national police force framework in 1839.
9. Dorothy Thompson, *The Chartists* (Temple Smith: London 1984) p. 133.
10. Dr Robert G. Hall has carried out extensive research into the Chartist movement in Ashton-under-Lyne and identified 65 activists from as early as 1838 in his article, *A United People? Leaders and Followers in a Chartist Locality 1838-48* (Journal of Social History 38(1) 2004, pp.179-203). Examples such as William Aitken and James Duke were to provide McDouall with strong support throughout.

CHAPTER FIVE

An Ardent Fiery Temperament

McDouall might have betrayed an element of nervousness speaking at that first meeting in Bury but he soon put the experience behind him. His passion for the cause was to grow so intense that within nine months, acting as delegate for Ashton-under-Lyne, he would become a highly articulate champion of Chartism on a national level. At the same time, he had also surfaced high up on the Home Office's unofficial 'wanted list'.

At this stage, having become a prominent figure in the public eye, it is possible to gain a much clearer idea of McDouall as a person: both in physical terms as well as the impression he made on others. RG Gammage indicates that 'McDouall was rather short, but possessed a straight and well-erected frame; in personal appearance he was decidedly handsome; his general features were extremely prepossessing; his mouth was small but well formed, void of any unpleasant compression of the lips, his face rather inclined to the oval; his eyes were full, and in moments of excitement sparkling and fiery; his brow was moderately high, very full and broad and his eyebrows dark and finely pencilled; his hair was light, approaching to sandy was parted in the centre and hung in long graceful curls behind his ears, and his whole appearance was highly interesting'.

As for McDouall's more general characteristics, Gammage commented that he was 'of an ardent, fiery temperament, and though naturally possessing strong reflective powers, was impulsive to the last degree, and by no means deficient in the quality of courage'.[1]

Someone else who witnessed him speaking on the platform was WE Adams, another Chartist who was later to write his memoirs. Adams commented on McDouall's 'picturesque figure' and style of attire, favouring black clothes and long cape which gave him 'the appearance of a hero of melodrama'. [2]

Returning for a moment to Gammage's pen portrait of McDouall, the only other evidence we have of his physical appearance comes from police sources which, in contrast to the Chartist historian's account, on one particular point of detail, give to believe that the colour of his hair was black. Certainly, the portrayals of him, such as the one in the National Gallery, appear to show his hair as dark-coloured. Perhaps he had developed ways of darkening its shade, in order to match his wearing of 'black clothes and long cape', and thereby enhance his theatrical presence on a public platform! Whatever the case, there is no doubting the powerful effect that McDouall's combined image and stage manner had on the audiences who came to see and listen to him.

In little more than months, McDouall's life became utterly transformed and in ways which carried an element of almost celebrity status. In constant demand to speak on platforms at demonstrations in the same manner as Stephens had been, he regularly found himself commanding the attention of thousands of people at a time.

He found himself enjoying a higher profile in other interesting ways. For example, McDouall could have hardly thought he might have become famous enough in such a short space of time to have had a portrait of himself produced. After all, it was usually only lords and politicians who were considered important enough for the purpose.

Then, no sooner had he managed to adjust to the larger setting of Ashton than he was pulled also in the direction of London.

∞

Another factor that had prompted Stephens to step down was because he recognised Ashton-under-Lyne needed to have someone to act as its delegate at the newly-constituted Chartist Convention in London, about to enter into permanent session from February 1839 onwards.

To McDouall, the opportunity to attend this assembly, taking place as it did in the capital, must have seemed a very exciting prospect. Set up as an 'alternative Parliament', it would have felt a great honour to be a member of this forum. McDouall would have known that the term 'Convention' was that given to the French Revolutionary parliament of the 1790s. In the new circumstances he found himself, he could have been forgiven for thinking he was on a fast track to playing a key role in the transformation of the way the country was run. Parallels might have sprung into his mind with French leaders like Robespierre and Danton who had become powerful figures with authority vested in them to launch radical programmes of social and political reform.

Unfortunately, however, the atmosphere he encountered in the London-based Chartist Convention of early 1839 didn't quite match up to its Parisian counterpart of yore. Far from being an insurgent central committee, the first meetings he attended were tame affairs, in effect run by delegates from London and Birmingham representing small artisan workshops. A pedestrian, bureaucratic tone prevailed, sticking closely to pre-arranged agendas rather than permitting any passionate, free-flow oratory

The founders of Chartism, such as William Lovett, set the pattern for the way business was conducted. Although the overall number of 53 delegates represented a large number of different constituencies and interests across the nation, it wasn't clear to McDouall how he was going to do proper justice to the rebel-rousing instincts of his constituents back in Ashton.

McDouall would not have been alone in feeling awkward and hamstrung. Many other delegates found the situation stifling and difficult to adapt to. Convention made little allowance for the fact that its members came with different concerns and priorities according to which area of the country they were representing. Quickly feeling frustrated, McDouall grasped the nettle and made immediate impact by breaking into agendas with stirring speeches that advocated the taking of 'ultimate measures', including the use of weapons, in order to bring about the realisation of Chartist aims.

However much the moderate elements would have recoiled in horror from the use of such expressions, many other delegates, especially those representing northern towns, knew exactly where McDouall was coming from. Ashton-under-Lyne itself was still very much under a spotlight after the recent, controversial arrest of Stephens in December. No-one would have needed reminding that Stephens had earned a reputation for coming across as a 'physical force' Chartist. It was only to be expected that any successor of his would pursue the same line.

In all these circumstances, McDouall felt committed to voicing the need for Convention to adopt extreme measures. Besides, he knew it wasn't just his own constituents who were feeling angry. Taking a militant stand reflected the way the pendulum was swinging in so many other places besides Ashton. Deeper economic depression had begun to take hold during 1838 and was set to bite even harder the following year.

Large-scale protest meetings, in the manner of the famous one that had taken place at Kersal Moor, were being staged in public venues across the country, bringing together disgruntled workers in their thousands. One for example taking place in Ramsbottom, regarded as a small town compared with many others in the broader Manchester area, had witnessed an estimated crowd of 5,000 people jamming themselves into Market Square. By way of response, the Government tried banning such events (stating that any attendance of 50 people or more constituted an illegal meeting) but, unable to police operations effectively, had ended up concentrating instead on a policy of arresting leaders, as initially in the case of Stephens. Despite showing some capacity to make arrests, custodians of law and order were still though finding it hard to maintain any overall semblance of control.

The situation was that many parts of the country, especially in northern textile towns, were in a state of turmoil by 4 February 1839 at the time the Convention began its deliberations in London. Posing a direct threat to the authority of Government, Chartist demonstrations, marches, together with arming and drilling had taken off on an unprecedented scale. Again using Ramsbottom as an example, a local Chartist leader, block-printer James Parkinson, headed demonstrations, 'and no less ardent, his wife, who, like Charlotte Corday, never lacked energy, took her place beside him, bearing conspicuously the 'cap of liberty'.

Husband and wife, James and Alice Parkinson, lived at 72, Bolton Street, only a few doors away from McDouall, who knew them very well. Hume Elliot, writing in 1893, adds that 'it is supposed that the leaden bullets dug up some years ago at 72, Bolton Street had been concealed by one of these of the advanced type'. [3]

∞

Determined to promote a strong line, McDouall was uncompromising in pushing forward the argument for insurrection. So adamantly did he commit himself to such a programme of action that he threatened to withdraw from Convention if it didn't give full endorsement to a call to arms. As well as speaking out at Convention, McDouall sought to air his views through the medium of newspapers. The development of Chartism coincided with a period when the power and influence of the printed word of newspapers was coming into its own. In the autumn of 1838, the moderate London Working Men's Association had supported the founding of a London-based newspaper, 'The Charter', to serve as the movement's mouthpiece.

Bearing in mind the Chartist Convention had started out in London, it made sense that this particular newspaper - the first copy of which had appeared on 27 January 1839 – should have been adopted by the Convention as its official news outlet. The aim had been to keep a nationwide audience updated on general developments but also to satisfy interest across all the different regions that were naturally keen to pick up on any particular contributions being made by their own locally-elected delegates. In reading-rooms and drinking-places all over the north, more literate individuals in the community took it upon themselves to share articles from 'The Charter' with those who would have struggled on their own to read them.

However, The Charter soon came under criticism from northern quarters for taking too passive a stance to events unfolding at the start of 1839. This dissatisfaction would prove a strong factor in The Charter losing revenue and ceasing publication little more than a year later in March 1840. Another factor in the demise of The Charter was the greater popularity of a competitor, 'The Northern Star'. This newspaper had started out life in 1837 as 'The Northern Star and Leeds General Advertiser' but when its proprietor Feargus O'Connor, a former Irish MP now intent on forging a career in English politics, switched focus to reporting on the Chartist movement, circulation numbers leapt from 10,000 in September 1838 to 50,000 in the early months of 1839, far outstripping the 6,000 copies sold per week of The Charter. Demand for the Northern Star was so great that a new two horsepower steam printing engine had to be installed on site to cope with demand. As an indication of the uptake the Northern Star had in factory-towns, 1,330 copies were ordered in Ashton alone in a week in February 1839. [4]

There were many aspects to the Northern Star which made it an instant hit with its readership. It was for example the first newspaper in British history to break free of the practice of devoting the front page to adverts. Instead, emphasis was given to rousing weekly 'letters' written by O'Connor himself, directly addressing issues of the moment. Another major selling-point was that different editions were brought out, tailored to different parts of the country. In addition, there was a letters page. Pen-portraits were presented of 'Chartist heroes' to readers avid to learn more about the background of leaders who represented them. The Star's poetry column invited contributions from Chartist activists.

As a delegate, McDouall was especially keen to ensure that his views and actions were prominent in newspapers. Even if this did not endear him to the authorities, who would have kept a covert eye on all Chartist media-forms, his newsworthiness went down very well with his Chartist supporters back in Ashton-under-Lyne. Regularly featuring in both The Charter and The Northern Star, although increasingly more the latter, it was not long before his firebrand style of expression succeeded in establishing McDouall's reputation further afield and helping to make him a household name amongst the ranks of the working class across the country.

Certainly, McDouall didn't need second invitations to see his name in print. As mentioned previously, he had inherited a penchant for poetry from his father back in Newton Stewart and lost no time in making the recently-crowned (1837) young monarch, Queen Victoria the subject of one of his poems. Addressing her in person, he signalled his hopes that Her Royal Highness would use her new position of power to alleviate the hardships being experienced by many of her less fortunate subjects. At the same time, he found it impossible to resist pointing out some of the ways in which her own splendid appearance at coronation contributed to this suffering, as shown in the lines quoted below:

That jewelled crown upon thy youthful head
Was chased and wrought by men who pine for bread.
The flowery lace, the silk, the satin traces

Were wove by hands all cramped by cold and pain.
Consumptive death rests on that needle-point,
And that small pin disturbs the infant's joints.

Although there were some, even among Chartist ranks, who would have considered the idea of addressing a poem to the Queen rather bold on McDouall's part, many more relished him putting pen to paper in this way. The poet himself justified the venture on the basis that it showed confidence on his part that people in power would in the end have conscience enough to take action on behalf of the nation's suffering mass of people. There is no record however of McDouall having received any official response either from or on behalf of Her Royal Highness!

Apart from strengthening his reputation as a spokesman for Chartism through various contributions to newspapers, McDouall also managed very quickly not only to pick up the skills of a journalist but also those potentially of an editor. All of which was to stand him in good stead for the time ahead when he was to start editing his own publication, the 'Chartist and Republican Journal' in 1841. The inclusion of the word 'Republican' in the title would suggest that by this point he had rather lost hope of active support for Chartism from the monarchy.

∞

As a sign of how revolutionary the times had suddenly become at the start of 1839, confidence built up amongst the McDouall camp of 'physical force' Chartists to the extent of an actual date being set for an armed insurrection to take place. Bearing out how Gammage described McDouall as having 'an ardent fiery temperament' and 'impulsive to the last degree', nothing exemplifies these characteristics so markedly as his hot-headed desire to mount an uprising against the government of the day. For McDouall, the stakes had spiralled out of recognition, in the matter of only three or four months, from measured criticisms of the Grants of Ramsbottom to emotive calls for revolution across the entire country.

Irrespective of how strong enthusiasm might have been in certain quarters in favour of such an undertaking, Convention was not about to give a green light to the motion. Taking account of the composition of the 53 delegates as a whole, a large percentage preferred to take a more cautious approach in expressing their sense of grievance. The tactics of this so-called 'moral force' wing of the movement would win the day leaving McDouall highly frustrated that his call for insurrection was rejected.

In the end, Convention voted in favour of presenting a petition to Parliament. As a tactic, there was some precedent for it having had success in France. The thinking was that if the government was faced with a document showing the movement had the support of hundreds of thousands of backers, the argument for political reform would become unanswerable. Not that the taking of a more passive line like this was ever going to convince McDouall, who 'declared that if the Convention was not to proceed to ulterior measures, he would go home at once'. [5]

Quite a few delegates though might have seen McDouall's threats of 'going home' as a form of emotional blackmail to force others at the Convention into pursuing a more militant line. Irrespective, the majority of the delegates still remained in favour of seeing whether the issue couldn't be resolved by more peaceable means. Irritatingly though, this involved a time-consuming process, trying to secure as many signatures as possible, prior to the petition being presented to Parliament. In addition to this hold-up, Convention had also taken a majority decision allowing Parliament to have proper time to consider its constitutional response to the document. Meanwhile, Convention's own proceedings dragged on in a vacuum, suffering from dwindling attendance.

Many were still left wondering what might have happened if the uprising, proposed by the 'physical force' group of delegates, with McDouall to the fore, had in fact taken place on the proposed date of 6 May? Evidence would appear to show that 'the government's defences were in a parlous state of disorganisation – the troops scattered in small detachments, the reinforcements from Ireland not yet arrived; the magistrates inert either from fear or indifference and the propertied inhabitants afraid to come forward as special constables to defend themselves'. [6]

However, in the light of the more conciliatory approach taken by Convention, the Government had taken advantage of inherent time-delays in the process to strengthen their defences against the threat that had at one point been raised of open insurrection. The police force was increased in size, as well as being augmented by enlistment of special constables, mainly being drawn from more middle-class roots. Plans were also hatched during this period of respite to prioritise planning for the arrest and imprisonment of vociferous Chartist ring-leaders.

Despite his call for an insurrection having been turned down in February, McDouall had not though carried out his threat to leave Convention. Instead, he had stayed on, continuing to relay his views, whilst at the same time taking part behind the scenes as a member of an influential group of delegates who remained advocates of the use of physical force. He may have felt a slight sense of consolation that, despite a majority of delegates having blocked his more radical method of protest, he was one of the leaders chosen to present the Chartist petition to Parliament. Fairly soon after the start of May, the petition was ready to be handed in at Westminster even though the actual presentation did not take place until 25 May 1839. Later, McDouall was to describe the experience on the day in the following, almost euphoric terms: 'There seemed to prevail a universal enthusiasm throughout the nation, and when the numbers were proclaimed, with 1,300,000 signatures, the cheers resounded'. [7]

In spite of the massive excitement generated on the day, any rush of expectation was curbed by having to wait now for a considered Government response. In the event, Parliament was destined to take the best part of two months to come to its decision on the matter. With little perceived reason to remain in London, Convention had re-convened in Birmingham on 13 May. At the top of its agenda was consideration of 'ulterior measures' to put to the people if the petition was rejected.

∞

Even though it was commonly agreed that pressure should continue to be exerted on Parliament, there were different views expressed as to how. Again, McDouall for his part was keen to adopt radical programmes of action. Dismissing the ideas the 'moral force' wing came up with - for example withdrawing savings from banks and boycotting hostile newspapers - as woefully inadequate, he urged the movement to call for a month-long strike in July, a so-called 'sacred month', when all work throughout the land would cease.

This idea gained considerable support at first. It wasn't the first time that a measure like this had been put forward by working class spokesmen. One William Benbow had been a longstanding advocate of using the weapon of a general strike to redress injustices perpetrated against workers. Benbow had written a pamphlet *The Grand National Holiday*, published in 1832, to explain the plan. Now seven years on, a majority of Chartist leaders were sufficiently convinced by the same type of argument for Convention to agree to go ahead with the idea of holding a 'sacred month' in July.

From the start though, preparatory steps to launch the 'sacred month' threw up major problems. Logistics would entail asking the few existing trade unions to provide financial support. However, most of them had little money in their coffers in the first place. They certainly didn't want to squander what they had on a notion that many viewed as a rash gamble. Although it was accepted that prolonged strike action would succeed in hurting the pockets of rich factory-owners, the greater number of Chartist leaders came to oppose the scheme on the basis that it would hit the smaller pockets of workers far harder, forcing them to the edge of starvation.

Throughout this time, McDouall continued to do whatever he could by way of putting his arguments forward in public. However, at the same time, he seems to have been increasingly drawn to taking steps behind the scenes. Frustrated by what he saw as a wasted period of inaction during the middle months of 1839, he became involved in clandestine arrangements to procure weapons for an armed uprising. He was a leading member of a 'secret committee' taking active steps to procure a strong enough supply of weapons that would lend stronger support to the idea that the 'physical force' argument had self-evident potential to succeed.

As stated earlier, the authorities had been seeking an opportunity to arrest 'physical force' Chartist leaders and bring them to account in the law-courts. McDouall, who must have been towards the top of the list, was one who was to be arrested. The given pretext, on the basis of charges of sedition and illegal assembly, was regarding his attendance at a meeting of an estimated 3,000 people in an area outside The Cotton Tree public house in the Lancashire town of Hyde. More precise charges were later to be revealed during McDouall's trial, scheduled to take place in August. Incidentally, The Cotton House had been opened in Hyde in 1830 and was so named as it coincided with the opening of the cotton mills in the Newton area by the Ashton brothers. By 1839, it had become a popular meeting place for local Chartists.

The exact circumstances involving McDouall's arrest were to be later described in memoirs written by his Chartist associate in Ashton-under-Lyne, William Aitken. After a tip-off that a warrant had been taken out for his arrest, McDouall happened to be staying overnight in Ashton at the time. However when the chief constable came to arrest him at the Commercial Hotel early the next morning, McDouall was already on his way to addressing a large meeting in Birmingham, in the celebrated Bull Ring.

Even if it only amounted to a delay in the process, it still gave some passing satisfaction to ardent supporters of McDouall's in the town, such as Aitken and Duke, knowing that they had contrived to foil an arrest intended to take place in Ashton. Aitken describes how he had arrived at the crack of dawn at the hotel where McDouall was staying and 'found him fast asleep. After awakening him I told him what was in the wind, what we had arranged to do, and with some slight persuasion he agreed to our plans. We came down stairs, got a glass of port negus each, and bowled off to Manchester post-haste'.

On their way to Manchester, Aitken reports 'the Doctor saying: "well if the warrant is out for my arrest I had better prepare for bail", and he gave us the name of a doctor in Bury, and a schoolmaster of the name of William Walker of Ramsbottom'. Aitken goes on to say that 'we arrived back in Bury in due time', having in the meantime packed McDouall off on a train to Convention headquarters in Birmingham, 'found the doctor, and informed him of our mission. He very politely refused, stating that although he admired the Doctor's abilities, yet if he were bound with him he should be identifying with his principles, a circumstance that he did not wish to do'. Although Aitken does not provide a name, the 'doctor in Bury' could well have been Matthew Fletcher. If so, perhaps McDouall might have been surprised at his refusal to assist in the matter. However, by this point in time, it has been commented elsewhere that 'poor Fletcher had had enough of Chartism...having got into troubled waters'. [8]

As Aitken continued, 'we then walked on to Ramsbottom, and found Mr Walker, arriving there at dinner time. We stated our case to him, and he at once complied saying, 'I always said the little devil would get himself into trouble, but damn him I'll be bound for him'. Meanwhile, 'the warrant that had been issued for McDouall's arrest was served on him the very first opportunity, and he and my esteemed friend, Mr John Bradley of Hyde, who was chairman at the meeting (on 22 April), where the Doctor had used the so-called seditious language, were arrested'. [9]

McDouall was not the only Chartist leader to be apprehended during this time. Although one of the first, a wave of more than 500 arrests, starting in June 1839, was to see influential figures in the movement, including William Lovett and Feargus O'Connor also taken out of commission. The government's ploy of arresting leaders was to prove highly effective because without proper leadership, those following the cause were left stranded and directionless.

∞

Whilst McDouall, and so many others, were awaiting trial, the dramatic and devastating news was announced on 12 July that Parliament had met that day in the House of Commons and rejected the Chartist petition submitted to them, back in May, by an overwhelming majority of 235 votes to 46. Chartism looked a beaten cause all round. Convention itself was now on the verge of collapse with increasing numbers of delegates having been arrested by the authorities.

McDouall spent considerable time preparing his defence in advance of the impending court case. Not that he could have held out much hope of success in gaining acquittal. He would have been painfully aware there wasn't a single case of anyone taken to court to date, on a charge similar to his own, who had escaped punitive sentence of one sort or another, either to prison in Britain or transportation to Australia.

During this same period, McDouall was further demoralised to learn that his brainchild of the 'sacred month' was on the rocks. More pain would come from reading in the Northern Star that its editor, Feargus O'Connor, had placed his considerable influence firmly on the side of those wanting to abort the strike action, arguing it would only lead to catastrophe and defeat. Perhaps more damagingly, the evidence O'Connor said he was drawing upon revealed that, apart from in the north-east, all other areas of England reported opposition to the proposal. It must have particularly irritated McDouall to read that even local areas of Manchester - which he would have seen as providing the backbone of support - were coming out against the strike call. In light of the general situation, the Chartist Convention resolved to rescind its previous decision and the 'sacred month' was called off on 22 July.

Such a decision also reflected the state of disarray Convention had been left in after the crushing news had come out ten days earlier that Parliament had rejected the Chartist petition. Indicative of the way in which strength had drained away from Convention, with much-reduced numbers of members participating, the vote to call off the 'sacred month' had been carried by 12 to 6, with 7 abstentions. These voting figures show how weakened in capacity Convention had become from its original total of 53 delegates. The justification for its continued existence was diminishing by the day. On 6 August, the 23 delegates remaining in office at this point suspended proceedings before the further decision was taken in early September for Convention to be dissolved.

Meanwhile, irrespective of the turbulence and fall-out around him, McDouall still remained intent on making a fight of it when his case came to court in August. He was determined to put up a defiant defence, both on his own account and the wider Chartist cause.

Notes on Sources

1. RG Gammage, *History of the Chartist Movement* (1854) p.67.
2. WE Adams, *Memoirs of a Social Atom* (1903) p212.
3. William Hume Elliot, *The Country and Church of the Cheeryble Brothers*, p. 134-5. N.B. Charlotte Corday (1768-93) was a figure of the French Revolution who was guillotined for murdering Jean-Paul Marat in his bath. Although Marat was a revolutionary too, she feared he was becoming too extremist for the good of the French people as a whole. In some ways though, a curious analogy for Hume Elliot to make with Alice Parkinson!
4. Northern Star, 23 February 1839.
5. Mark Hovell, *The Chartist Movement* (Manchester, 1918) p. 125.
6. FC Mather, *The Government and the Chartists in Chartist Studies*, edited by Asa Briggs (1959) p.380.
7. *Peter Murray McDouall, Chartist and Republican Journal*: 17 April 1841.
8. Hovell, *The Chartist Movement* p.168.
9. The main section of events described here, leading up to McDouall's arrest is taken from William Aitken, *Remembrances and Struggles of a Working Man for Bread and Liberty* pp. 34-5 - published by Tameside Leisure Services: Libraries and Heritage (1996)

CHAPTER SIX

Marry the Turnkey's Daughter.

Facing charges of sedition and illegal assembly, Peter Murray McDouall's court case took place at Chester Assizes on 16 August 1839. [1]

Presiding judge on the day was Baron Gurney. In his 70s, he was notable for being the last judge to have passed a sentence of capital punishment for sodomy, convicting James Pratt and John Smith under section 15 of the Offences against the Person Act 1828, which had replaced the Buggery Act of 1533.

The Attorney General prosecuting on the occasion was Mr. Hill. The prosecution case rested on the assertion that, at a meeting taking place on 22 April in the Lancashire town of Hyde, McDouall's declared object had been 'to overthrow laws by force, and to incite the people to bloody revolution'. It was further maintained that, along with several accomplices, he had purchased muskets and bayonets from George Thompson, a Birmingham gunsmith, besides placing orders for many more.

The first of the two formal charges brought forward was that of sedition on McDouall's part. The prosecution case relied primarily on the evidence of John Gatley whose status was referred to as 'Constable of Hyde'. Called by Hill to testify, Gatley stated that McDouall had told his audience at the Hyde meeting that '50 determined people could capture the country: all that was necessary was to seize the arms at the Tower of London and distribute the weapons to 200,000 Londoners'. Further incriminating evidence was supplied by Gatley, purporting to give exact detail of what McDouall said at the meeting.

When it came to the defendant's turn to cross-examine this witness, McDouall posed the question as to how Gatley could be so confident about being able to quote word-for-word what he had said on 22 April. The prosecution case was weakened when Gatley admitted he hadn't taken any notes at the time but waited until the day after to write his recollections down on paper. Nevertheless, it was unlikely the jury had any qualms in trusting to the gist of what Gatley had reported back on.

The second charge was in relation to 'illegal assembly'. In reply, McDouall denied the Hyde meeting had been illegal. In his words, 'the people merely met together for the purpose of considering the expediency of adopting the People's Charter'. He did not deny, however, advocating the possession of weapons, asserting that people had a right to carry arms, not least for self-defence against tyranny, curbing the repressive powers of the state. This was an argument often made in Chartist circles, most notably in the past by Stephens, but a dubious one to put forward in the present circumstances.

Unquestionably, it would have been self-incriminating if McDouall had indeed spoken at a crowded public meeting about seizing control of the Tower of London, almost as if seeking to re-enact the 1789 Storming of the Bastille. Whatever had been the exact form of words used at this meeting, it would have been hard for McDouall to have claimed he was innocent on the question of procuring weapons for proactive use in support of the Chartist cause. Besides, Birmingham gunsmith George Thompson had already confessed to selling muskets and bayonets to McDouall. The Home Office was in possession of a sworn deposition by Thompson stating that on 9 May 'McDouall and a certain James Duke, of Ashton-under-Lyne, were in Birmingham ordering a score of muskets and bayonets to be sent to the latter's home in Ashton, and promising an order for several hundred more if these were approved'.

Compounding this, various Chartists from Ashton-under-Lyne had been caught red-handed with a large quantity of these firearms in their possession - many more than might have been considered necessary for 'self-defence' - and were to appear in due course before these same Assizes on such a charge.

Hill seemed determined to say everything he could to discredit McDouall's personal motivation in 'inciting the people to bloody revolution'. He lost no opportunity to point out the dangers to the existing order of society from the working classes being whipped up to insurrection after listening to the likes of McDouall. Two particular sections of his delivery notably illustrate the message he was trying to impress on judge and jury:

'The effect produced by the speeches of men like McDouall had been to set the workmen against their masters; and after having deluded the poor people by unfounded hopes, they expected to reap an advantage out of the confusion they would create'.

Equally provocatively, Hill said of McDouall: 'He formerly was a surgeon, but finding the trade of agitation more profitable or more likely to lead to his advantage, he had forsaken his profession, and lent his aid to produce dissatisfaction amongst the people, and confusion in the country, expecting amidst the general scramble to secure something for himself'.

McDouall though was not one to let such comments pass unanswered. Immediately, he had responded with fierce indignation: 'I loudly protest against the Attorney General declaring that I could only have one object in view and that of the worst description – an object in filling my pockets at the expense of the poor'.

The defendant was not about to go quietly! He was intent on projecting the strongest case he could. Even if he knew it wouldn't cut much ice with judge and jury, at least it would resonate well with the defendant's cheering chorus of supporters present in the crowded court-room. Determined to launch a counter-blast of his own, feeling no doubt he had weathered the storm of Hill's personal accusations, he now mounted his own powerful response. One that he had obviously taken a lot of trouble to prepare in advance. Court records show that he went on to speak for a length of more than four hours in justification both of himself and the broader cause of Chartism. To start with, he engaged in an extended preamble regarding the importance of adhering to 'Britain's ancient constitution'. The People's Charter, he argued, was only restoring rights that had been granted under Magna Carta but snatched away since.

Next, he concentrated on exposing conditions in the manufacturing districts 'to which he attributed the agitation commenced by (the working classes) for the increase of their political power'. On this topic, he described what he had seen for himself of the effects over time from the introduction of the factory system, making reference to his boyhood experience in Newton Stewart observing how the experience and life-style of handloom weavers had been ruined by the introduction of factories. Further, he cited details from the paper he had delivered to the British Association, the year before in Newcastle, which had highlighted the adverse conditions affecting cotton-workers in Ramsbottom.

Moving the spotlight further afield, in case it should be thought he was only talking about the local area surrounding his medical practice, McDouall then quoted instances of deprivation in the Hyde area, noting the instance of a man who had to keep a family of nine on a wage of 11 shillings and seven pence per week, and others who were so overcrowded that they slept seven to a bed. 'If people were comfortable, there would be no agitation', he pressed, 'but if real misery and distress exists, then agitation was the mere effect and their suffering the cause of the agitation. The wrongs which people had to endure could only be ended, McDouall stressed, once they had a say in the government of the country'.

Citing many individual cases of people and families suffering at the present time, McDouall argued the Chartist case long and hard to judge and jury, insisting it did not threaten the existing order of society in terms of property and possessions, but merely sought a degree of fairer political representation:

'My Lord and Gentlemen, the division we desire, is not one of property or the possessions of others, but what we want is a division of political rights, of which we have been unjustly deprived, and which are now unequally divided. The great producing class are deprived of any voice in the representation, whilst the whole balance of power rests in the hands of those who are the mere distributors of the produce of others' industry'.

Above all else, McDouall set out to make out what he thought should come across as a reasonable case:

'My Lord and Gentlemen, I do not ask for anything that is visionary in theory, or unattainable in practice. I ask for what had existed before; for what exists now on a splendid scale in America'.

Lastly, McDouall wanted to defend himself against the accusation that he had somehow deluded the working classes into entertaining false hopes of betterment:

'My Lord and Gentlemen, I have never taught people to expect a pictured Utopia, a splendid fairy-land of idleness and comfort. I have ever taught them to look for, and demand good wages for their labour'.

∞

Eye-witness accounts reveal the impression the defendant made in court on 16 August. For example, according to William Aitken, who was seated in the courtroom gallery that day, McDouall conducted himself 'with a firmness and an eloquence which even his enemies could not but admire. There was no shrinking before that high tribunal from the principles that he had advocated'.

At the same time, it had particularly galled Aitken to hear the Attorney General vilifying his friend in court by accusing him of exploiting workers for financial gain. Aitken, as he was to put forward in his memoirs, firmly believed that McDouall not only acted altruistically in all his dealings but that he had actually made huge personal sacrifices in his efforts to support the cause of the working class:

'McDouall had, when elected to the Convention, a very good practice where he resided, another freehold property in Scotland, that belonged to him, two sisters and his mother, besides a good round sum of money in the Bury Bank. The Chartists of this locality (Ashton-under-Lyne) were to pay him a pound a day while sitting on that Convention, but I am sorry to say they never did, but he still continued in London, and going about the country advocating the principles of democracy, till his banking account was used up. Yet we were told (at the 1839 trial) that these agitators, these disturbers of the public peace were making money out of their dupes'. [2]

On the question of property back in Newton Stewart, since becoming a Chartist delegate, McDouall had sold a dwelling-house, barn and stable, raising £409 in order to give him much-needed cash in hand to cover the expenses he was incurring.

Back to the impression McDouall had made at his trial, Thomas Dunning, another Chartist who had witnessed court proceedings, described how after the trial: 'I had called in at the Bull Head's Tavern, Northgate Street…and among the assembled company I found a party of special constables…who were ordering jugs of ale and drinking the health of Doctor McDouall, whose speech in defence had converted them to Chartism'. [3]

However, the defendant's speech cannot have had quite the same effect on the jury who had convicted McDouall of the charges without bothering to retire! Perhaps they thought they had had enough already after enduring a four-hour harangue from him. As for Judge Gurney, he ended up recommending a sentence of twelve months' imprisonment on McDouall. This amounted to six months fewer though than the sentences imposed on the four Ashton Chartists caught in possession of the firearms. Not that any difference in lengths of sentence would have affected the strong bond between McDouall and his constituents.

Which was just as well because all of them were going to spend time, on Her Majesty's pleasure, in the same gaol at nearby Chester Castle. Incidentally, Birmingham gunsmith Thompson, found guilty of a charge of conspiracy, was sentenced to eighteen months there too. Given that he had furnished the prosecution with written evidence against McDouall and his Ashton followers, he was not to relish being the butt of their hostility.

∞

For a variety of other reasons, McDouall's stay in prison was not to pass uneventfully. Another of his fellow-inmates was the Rev. Joseph Rayner Stephens, who of course had been McDouall's mentor at the time he had succeeded him as Ashton delegate to Convention at the start of 1839. Despite this, the relationship between the two had become acrimonious long before they rubbed shoulders again within the confines of Chester Gaol.

In recent months, an intense rivalry had sprung up between these two strong personalities, each apparently vying against one another to win the hearts and minds of Ashtonians. Both men might have been said to have their own cult followings. However, over the course of the last few months, McDouall had succeeded in winning over to his side many followers who had once been ardent disciples of Stephens. Perhaps this was only to have been expected in the light of Stephens having stood down following his arrest in December 1838. Even so, Stephens, the older man by a margin of ten years, may have harboured a bit of jealousy that his one-time protege had proved quite so adept and successful in the meantime, as well as seeming to more than match his mentor in terms of personal charisma on the speaking podium.

Then there had been the contrasting approach taken by the two in their respective courtroom trials. While McDouall had gone into his own with all guns blazing, ever more fervent and proud of his identification with Chartism, Stephens had come across almost apologetically, claiming he had only ever become involved with the movement based on concerns over the effects of the factory system. To be fair, this might have been how McDouall too had come to Chartism, but the glaring difference between them now was that one defendant championed the cause to the hilt while the other seemed to be shrinking back. Many suspected that Stephens was just trying to save his skin. Much good it had done with the judge passing an eighteen-month sentence on him. However, an apparent concession made was that he should be able to enjoy certain privileges during confinement over and above those normally granted to prisoners.

Another aspect relating to Stephens' trial, which had rankled with Ashton Chartists, was that, having contributed to his defence fund, it had added insult to injury when he had not sought to defend himself as a self-avowed Chartist, appearing more than willing to distance himself from the cause. However, a more visceral source of contention between McDouall and Stephens had arisen when in June 1839 McDouall had publicly accused Stephens of having committed an indecent assault on a woman, identifying her as the unmarried sister of a Chartist leader by the name of James Bronterre O'Brien. Though the allegation was never proven, it could not help but sully Stephens' reputation. Certainly it was to terminate any shred of remaining trust between the two of them. It was said that, following this accusation, Stephens' hatred for McDouall 'had no bounds'. [4]

There were many prisoners in Chester Gaol at this time coming from Ashton, who basically split into two factions - those who followed Stephens and those who followed McDouall. There was a report of violence having taken place when one prisoner had sustained a broken jaw. Stephens was the one much more troubled by all the tensions that arose. In a recorded statement to a gaol inspector, he commented that: 'I have been insulted by one set of Chartists here, who sided with McDouall, although I have in frequent instances given them food and money'. [5]

On the question of food and money though, it would have been an added cause of resentment that while virtually everyone else was under lock and key in confined spaces, Stephens was not only allowed to maintain himself with access to outside providers but was also granted a private room to study and eat. It appears to have been possible, within the way Chester Gaol operated, for certain prisoners to enjoy greater privileges due to their social class. Which was another reason why Stephens became so hated among the pro-McDouall faction. While as a doctor, McDouall would have been eligible for more privileged status, he by contrast had made it something of a badge of honour to live under the same more stringent conditions as his band of supporters.

Most prominent in this group now supporting McDouall was James Duke. At the age of 36, he was married with six children. Just how his prison sentence squared with domestic considerations is not clear. It is evident though he had few qualms about having signed up to the Chartist cause with all the family deprivations the commitment had entailed. A cotton spinner by profession, he was also the landlord of the Bush Inn, Stamford Street, Ashton-under-Lyne. This pub had been a well-known meeting-place from the start for Chartists. It was here that Stephens had been arrested by the Bow Street Runner, Henry Goddard.

Meanwhile, perhaps by way of getting his own back for the accusation of indecent assault, Stephens had sought to expose what he interpreted as McDouall's own immorality, alleging that he had tried to seduce 'the turnkey's daughter' here in Chester Gaol itself. This counter-accusation though wasn't to have the sting Stephens had been hoping for. While it was true that a relationship had developed between McDouall and the daughter of one of the warders, it was one though which was destined to be lasting. When eventually he was released from Chester Gaol, he and Mary Ann were to travel up to Glasgow to get married.

Incidentally, this was not to be the only example of Chartist prisoners finding themselves caught up in romance (albeit in the unlikely setting of incarceration) and ending in marriage. In another case, that of James Williams, a Chartist leader in the north-east of England, he had entered into a relationship with a wealthy young lady who, as part of her charitable work, acted as a prison visitor. Eventually on release, they had married. With her financial assistance, Williams had opened a printing business which was later to develop into the 'Sunderland Herald'.

Given that her father was a poorly-paid warden, Mary Ann had rather less to offer in pecuniary terms. Not that this made any difference as far as their joint commitment to a shared future was concerned. Although the road ahead was to prove ever more onerous, Mary Ann was always to stand by her husband in his on-going struggles to fight the cause of Chartism.

∞

News of what was going on around the country filtered through to McDouall in prison. For example, of an armed uprising that had taken place in Wales in November 1839. It was clear that the venture had not turned out well.

On the night of 3/4 November, leader John Frost had led several thousand marchers from surrounding regions of South Wales, many of whom had weapons including rifles, towards the town of Newport. The next day they had marched on the town's Westgate Hotel, where the police and mayor were keeping several prominent Chartists under lock and key. It seems that Frost and other local leaders were intending to seize control of the town and trigger a national uprising. Unknown to the force arriving at the hotel, a small detachment of infantrymen were occupying the building. As the demonstrators massed outside, seeking to free the prisoners, a gun went off, possibly by accident. In any case, it prompted the soldiers to fire their rifles. Some Chartists broke into the hotel but were shot at again. In chaos and disarray, the crowd had eventually dispersed, but with casualties of 22 dead and many more wounded. The leaders were to stand trial a few months later.

Writing a letter from prison, McDouall acknowledged the uprising's main leader – John Frost – as a personal friend, but argued it had been an 'ill-managed, foolish and quixotic adventure'. Not that the insurrection in Newport was the last such at this time. Samuel Holberry led an abortive rising in Sheffield on 12 January 1840. Two weeks later, on 26 January, Robert Peddie attempted similar action in Bradford. On both occasions, spies had kept magistrates aware of the conspirators' plans, and each of these attempted uprisings had been easily quashed.

Meanwhile in Wales, Frost and the other two main leaders of the Newport Rising, Zephaniah Williams and William Jones, were found guilty of high treason and sentenced to be 'hanged, drawn and quartered', incidentally the last time in history that this particular sentence was passed. Eventually, the sentence was commuted to transportation to Australia.

For their parts, Holberry and Peddie received long prison sentences with hard labour. Holberry died of consumption in prison at York Castle on 21 June 1842 aged 27. Honoured as a martyr to the cause, he was buried in Sheffield General Cemetery with an estimated 50,000 Chartist supporters attending his funeral.

∞

McDouall was still able to maintain outside contact with others by means of written correspondence. However, such letters would have been heavily vetted by the prison authorities. The reality was that, from the time he became a prisoner in Chester Gaol, his role and influence was inevitably diminished and in abeyance until his twelve-month prison sentence came to an end.

As this time drew nearer, his thoughts must have increasingly concentrated on what he would seek to do when free again. There were serious questions he would need to take into consideration. For example, how far might he commit himself again to playing the same prominent role as before, addressing meetings around the country? Or perhaps cut his losses and return to conducting his medical practice in Ramsbottom, the town where he had started out his career as a practising doctor in 1835? There is no evidence to show at this point that McDouall was thinking of abandoning or trying to sell off his medical practice at 18 Bolton Street.

Irrespective of all that had changed in his life over the last two years, McDouall was still concerned about how workers around Ramsbottom, and particularly in Nuttall village, were coping at the onset of a new decade – sadly starting out with no greater hope of prosperity – to become known later as 'The Hungry Forties'.

∞

All of which makes it interesting to see how the Grant Brothers themselves had fared during these more troublesome times of the late 1830s. How had they faced all the new tensions breaking out? Plus, in the context of McDouall ending up in prison, what would they have made of such news? More than likely, they would have concluded he had it coming to him!

If one holds to what Hume Elliot has to say on such matters, it would appear that the Grants at all times sought to confine themselves to business matters. Daniel, 'after an early experience, avoided political meetings'. In essence, such an aversion appears to have stemmed from a particular meeting in Manchester, explained as follows to the biographer in a letter sent to him years later by Daniel's grand-niece. 'To a gentleman present who was on the opposite side, Daniel Grant said something very severe. The gentleman said: Oh! Mr Grant, you break a man's head and then put a plaster on it to make it well. He told me he felt the rebuke so keenly that he left the room never again to be present at a public meeting'. [6]

∞

By 1838, William's state of health had become a cause for concern to the extent that Daniel had taken it upon himself to go and live permanently with him at Springside. Where did this leave him in his relationship with Elizabeth Brereton in his town mansion house on Mosley Street?

At the same time as committing himself to joining his elder brother at Springside, Daniel seems to have taken certain other decisive steps in his life at this point. One of which involved Elizabeth and the two boys, Daniel and Charles, being found accommodation at 45 Burlington Street, Greenheys, where her name appeared in the Manchester directories of the time as 'Mrs Elizabeth BRERETON'.

From then on, the relationship between Daniel and Elizabeth seems to have waned. Nevertheless, it is clear that Daniel did not disown himself entirely from the boys. Even if, in various ways, it may have seemed an increasing tight-rope he was walking, he continued to take a dutiful interest in the welfare of his two sons. For example, in 1842, his elder son Daniel Grant, about 17 years of age now, appears to be able to visit Springside and mix freely with Daniel's nephew and niece. Meanwhile, younger brother Charles, noted to be prone to epileptic fits, may not have visited so often. In the 1841 census return for Burlington Street, both are described as 'scholars'. [7]

∞

Life at Springside was not without frissons of its own, as Hume Elliot describes:

'One evening, the two of them were quietly seated in Springside when a visitor was announced, wishing to see Mr. Grant. In a short time, after William had undertaken to meet with this visitor on his own, Daniel had heard loud and threatening words from a strange voice…demanding money'. Knowing his brother not to be in the best of health, he becomes very concerned.

Hume Elliot goes on to describe how the intrepid Daniel 'on entering, took in the situation at a glance, and walking right up to the fellow with a burst of indignation seized him by the collar. A sudden movement of the man's hand showed that he was armed. Daniel caught sight of a pistol. With almost super-human strength he forced the fellow down the long hall and through the smaller one to the veranda, and there took from him two pistols and a dagger. He then marched him down to the side of the little lake in front of the house, and flung the pistols and dagger right into the middle of it, and ordered the intruder off'. Such it appears was how, on this particular occasion, the 'physical-force' threats of the times were faced down within the confines of Springside.

Regarding any more extended Grant 'take' on political matters, according to Hume Elliot, 'they were opponents of the Corn Bill in the year of Waterloo, and continued generous contributors to the agitation directed against the Corn Laws until their repeal in 1846'.[8]

∞

The Grants had no doubt been pleased to have heard of the founding of the nationwide Anti-Corn Law League in 1838, combining all the local associations that had been set up in earlier years. With the League headquarters being set up in Manchester, they would have been only too keen to give active support to the movement. As factory-owners, the Grants would have been rightly concerned for their workers over the fact it had been more costly for so long for them to buy bread. It hadn't meant though that they would have been philanthropic enough to compensate for this in terms of raising wages.

However, the Grants would probably have considered themselves very caring in other more random, spontaneous acts of charity. For example, 'a pastime of perennial glee to Daniel was scattering, it was called "perrying", handfuls of money among the youngsters, as he drove to town'. He appears to have heartily enjoyed, almost like a circus impresario might have done, 'the eager athletic feats of the lads, tumbling over one another in their scramble for the coins, as they shouted "Grants for ever! Grants for ever!" Meanwhile, the more frugal William had commented on one of these occasions: 'Ah, Daniel, Daniel! I have seen the day when you had to work very hard for the money you are now throwing away!' [9]

Their journeys to and from Manchester provided quite a spectacle. The Grant carriage was drawn by two dapple grey horses and both the coachman and the footman wore green livery with gold braid. There were also two Dalmatian dogs to match the horses and these ran behind.

Hume Elliot comments of the Grants generally that 'there was nothing in their lives when it was their lot to be poor which caused them to be ashamed when it was their fortune to become rich'. Giving added emphasis to this way of thinking is a story the biographer tells, as stated by William himself, as to how a man once sought to insult him in a public place by saying, "I believe, Mr Grant you were very poor when you came to these parts." "Oh, yes," said William, "I was very poor, and if it had been you, you would have remained poor." [10]

The Grants never had much sympathy for anyone complaining about poverty, believing it was up to each individual to do something to escape the trap. Nor did they have any time for the cause of Chartism. Workers knew they could be sacked if they were seen bringing a Northern Star newspaper to work with them. With Chartism having become much more of a threat from 1839 onwards, the Grants would have been relieved that the government took the actions they had, arresting and locking up leading troublemakers like 'Ramsbottom's young doctor'.

∞

As for McDouall himself, even if his scope for action had been curtailed by his one-year spell in custody, making him a little more cautious in the meantime about advocating physical force, it soon became clear on release he was anything but penitent. Instead, he seemed more motivated than ever to champion the cause of Chartism.

NOTES ON SOURCES

1. The account, in this chapter, of McDouall's trial at Chester Assizes, taking place on 16 August 1839, is based on a transcript of proceedings which is available for viewing at Tameside Local Studies Archive Centre in Ashton-under-Lyne.

2. William Aitken, *Remembrances*, pp 38-9.

3. *The Reminiscences of Thomas Dunning, Testaments of Radicalism*, edited by David Vincent, pp 139-140.

4. MS Edwards, *Purge This Realm: A Life of Joseph Rayner Stephens* (Epworth Press: 1994) p 93.

5. A telling account of the acrimony between Stephens and McDouall, and their respective supporters, is provided in an article by Derek Pattison, *Portraits of Political Prisoners in 1841* - Manchester Radical History Portal. N.B. Although the title refers only to the year 1841 (McDouall had been released from his one-year sentence in August 1840), the article does in fact cover the whole period from 1839 onwards when Stephens, McDouall, together with those Ashton Chartists found guilty of firearms possession, started their prison sentences together at Chester.

6. William Hume Elliot, *The Story of The Cheeryble Grants* (1906) p. 176.

7. Alan Hitch, *Daniel Grant, Famous or Infamous?* – (Ramsbottom Heritage Society News Magazine No. 30 Spring 2006) p.11

8. Hume Elliot, *The Story of The Cheeryble Grants* pp. 157-9.

9. Ibid: p. 162.

10. Ibid: p. 125.

ILLUSTRATIONS

Portrait of Peter Murray McDouall 1840
engraving courtesy of RG Gammage, History of the Chartist
Movement 1837-1853, (second edition in 1894) p. 156.

Blue plaque dedicated to Peter Murray McDouall
photo courtesy of Ramsbottom Heritage Society.

Portrait of William Grant – photo of engraving
courtesy of Donald MacBeth, Artists and Illustrators, London:
item from Rev. RR Carmyllie collection, Bury Library Archives.

Portrait of Daniel Grant – photo of engraving
courtesy of Donald MacBeth, Artists and Illustrators, London:
item from Rev. RR Carmyllie collection, Bury Library Archives.

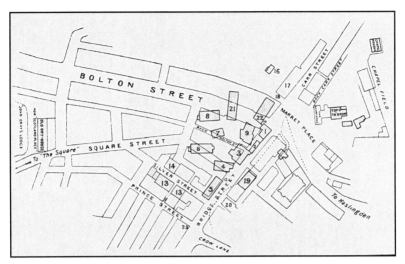

Map of "Old Ground", Ramsbottom – courtesy of William
Hume Elliott, The Country and Church of the Cheeryble Grants
(George Lewis and Sons, Selkirk, 1893) opposite p. 112.

Grants Tower (prior to collapse in 1944) – photo courtesy of
Rev. RR Carmyllie collection, Bury Library Archives.

Members of the Chartist National Convention 1839
image courtesy of Stock Image – Science Photo Library.

Blue plaque: The Cotton Tree Public House in Hyde –
commemorating Joseph Rayner Stephens, PM McDouall and
John Bradley – courtesy of Open Plaques, photo by author.

Newport Rising – 'The attack of the Chartists on
the Westgate Hotel, Newport, November 4th 1839' –
image of drawing courtesy of Wikipedia.

Portrait of Rev. Joseph Rayner Stephens –
courtesy of Spartacus Educational.

The 1842 Petition being carried to Westminster –
contemporary print courtesy of National Archives UK.

Preston: 'Attack on the military': Two Rioters Shot –
print courtesy of Illustrated London News 1842.

£100
REWARD.

Whereas,

A WARRANT has been issued for the APPREHENSION of
PETER MURRAY McDOUALL, late of Ramsbottom,
near Bury, Surgeon; he is better known by the name of

DR. McDOUALL,

CHARTIST LECTURER.

DESCRIPTION.

He is about 27 years of age, stands about 5 ft. 6 in. high,
inclined to be stout, has long dark hair, swarthy complexion,
with high cheek bones, sharp black eyes, whiskers rather
lighter than his hair; generally dresses in black; speaks
quick, with a Scotch accent.

The above Reward will be paid by the Government to
any Person who shall give such Information as will lead to
the Apprehension of the said Peter Murray McDouall.

*Information to be given to Sir CHARLES SHAW,
Chief Commissioner of the Manchester Police.*

TOWN HALL, MANCHESTER,
September 3rd, 1842.

SIMPSON AND GILLETT, PRINTERS, MARKET STREET, MANCHESTER

Offer of reward for Peter McDouall

Offer of Reward for Dr McDouall – courtesy of M. Jenkins,
The General Strike of 1842, (London 1980) p 231.

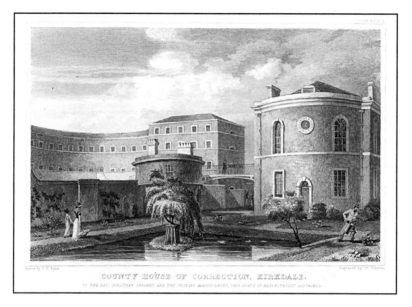

County House of Correction, Kirkdale – engraving by
W. Watkins – courtesy of Lancashire Illustrated 1831.

1848's Chartist Rally on Kennington Common –
courtesy of Love Lambeth: Lambeth Council.

Portrait of Feargus O'Connor – courtesy of
the University of Nottingham.

1854 Eureka Rebellion - attack on stockade - image
of drawing courtesy of Wikipedia.

Portrait of William Aitken – courtesy of
Tameside Local Studies Library, Ashton.

Peel Tower, Ramsbottom – courtesy of Dronestagram.

CHAPTER SEVEN

'Pills, Pamphlets and Politics'.

Released from Chester prison on 13 August 1840, McDouall was feted at a succession of 'liberation' events. All his various supporters, still remembering his speech from the dock, were keen to have the chance to catch up on his spellbinding oratory again. Immediately though, he looked to have put himself back in deep water. Drawing quite a crowd, his first meeting had come to the notice of the local magistrates who declared it an illegal assembly and ordered the police to break up proceedings.

Going back to Dunning's description of how the special constables said they were converted to Chartism after hearing McDouall speak, many still had sympathy and were slow to act on orders. Fearing a conflict that might provide the authorities with a pretext for re-arresting him, McDouall took it upon himself to abandon the meeting. At the same time, it must have been heartening to have felt he had the police and soldiers on his side. Such was McDouall's celebrity status that he was invited to attend meetings in other parts of the north-west. His first had been at the Queen's Theatre, Liverpool, where 'one of the largest meetings which had ever taken place in the town' was held. [1]

Just as remarkable, soon after, was the meeting at the Carpenters' Hall in Manchester. A large procession had set off from the city-centre to meet McDouall's train when it arrived at Cross Lane station, Salford. Most of the marchers were trade unionists and Chartist radicals. At the front of the procession, a portrait of McDouall was held aloft bearing the inscription: 'The Tyrant's Foe'.

However provocative this meeting might have appeared to the authorities, there is no evidence of any official action being taken to halt it, let alone arrest anyone. Perhaps he was living something of a charmed life but it didn't stop McDouall embarking again on wide-ranging tours, addressing a whole host of venues in the Chartist cause. At the Manchester meeting, McDouall had made it clear that imprisonment had quenched nothing of his ardour for the cause. After his release, McDouall managed to fit in twenty-seven meetings starting out in Chester, moving on into Lancashire, Yorkshire and thence onwards into Scotland.

Added to this, he and Mary Ann were to take the opportunity to get married while they were in Glasgow. McDouall seemed determined their marriage should take place under Scottish law. Feeling an innate distaste for the kind of 'Churchism' which characterised the English form of nuptial procedure, he much preferred the Scottish version with its emphasis on the principle of mutual consent of partners as opposed to going along with the dictates of a strictly formalised religious service.

As far as his Chartist involvement was concerned, the highlight was to come on 21 September in Glasgow at an event where an estimated 200,000 people assembled to hear invited speakers, with McDouall playing a principal role alongside other leaders, White and Collins. A huge procession had headed for Glasgow Green, with 30 bands playing and 100 banners held aloft, adding atmosphere and colour to the occasion. Workers marched in their trade groups of all descriptions, including for example masons, smiths, shoemakers, cabinetmakers, dyers, dressers, boilermakers and many others. Female Chartist supporters made up another contingent of their own.

In the more suppressed post-1839 climate, Scotland was one of the few remaining places where mass demonstrations were still taking place. Happy as McDouall would have been to have chance to be speaking in a livelier Scottish setting, he still must have felt the need for a certain restraint in what he said. Even if his oratorical style had lost none of its fervour, an examination of the content of the speeches he made showed a measured sense of reflection. For example, his attitude to 'physical force' was much more moderate-sounding

As he told the Edinburgh gathering on 24 September: 'We gave our passions the rein; but you have been more cautious, you have suffered less – you gave the reins to reason'. This was not quite the same as saying he had renounced the use of force altogether. Incidentally, at this meeting in Edinburgh, he had prefaced his remarks on the subject by expressing pride to his audience that his grandfather had fought against British troops alongside George Washington in the American War of Independence. [2]

What he now advocated was the possession of weapons for purely defensive purposes. Certain opinion may have attributed McDouall's latest, more circumspect stance to the fact his hands were now rather more tied, through having been bound over for five years to keep the peace.

∞

Many Chartists, including McDouall, were keen to re-structure the way the movement was organised. Against the background of the recent setbacks suffered in Newport, Sheffield and Bradford, an urgent need was felt to replace the now defunct National Convention with a new body that would provide greater coherence and sense of unity. The argument developed that the process by which the 1839 Chartist Convention was formed had been seriously flawed. Managing only to create a loose form of pressure group politics, it was judged to have been ineffective. A fresh start was made in the later months of 1840. A new organisation was established, the National Charter Association, aimed at having a much more clearly defined membership structure and set of rules.

From the outset, McDouall played a prominent part in its formation. It is interesting to note, from the ranks of those serving on the original Convention at the start of 1839, he was one of very few to be putting himself forward again now. The large turnover in leading personnel can be attributed to a variety of factors, such as general demoralisation following the defeats of 1839, plus the enforced absence of key individuals like O'Connor (still detained in York Castle serving his 18-month gaol sentence), Frost and many others besides.

An early priority for the NCA in its reconstituted form was to maintain the campaign for a pardon for leaders of the Newport Rising, John Frost, Zephaniah Williams and William Jones. Over the spring of 1841, 1,339,298 signatures were collected for a petition that not only sought pardons for 'The Newport Three' but at the same time also called again upon the House of Commons to accept the People's Charter.

On 25 May, the petition was presented to Parliament by Thomas Duncombe, MP for Finsbury in NE London, a radical politician who was to prove a stalwart in championing the Chartist cause over future years. One newspaper report described the scene as events unfolded in Parliament: 'the petition was presented, the debate began, finally a bell rang, and the Speaker cried out clear the gallery'.

At this point, the gallery was packed with Chartists come to witness proceedings. However, to continue with the report:

'All strangers rushed out, the doors were bolted, and whilst murmurs of anxiety filled the passages, the bolts creaked again, and out rushed the members.

"How has it gone sir?"

"Votes equal, 58 and 58"

"How has the Speaker given it?"

"Against".

"Damn him". [3]

In this manner, the less well-remembered petition of 1841 was rejected by the House of Commons albeit only on the casting vote of the Speaker.

∞

For Chartist leaders seeking to maintain engagement, there was also the headache as to how, without massive private source of income, anyone could cope financially with the role. Originally the idea had been that constituents would subscribe towards delegates' cost of living but as Aitken had said of McDouall's own situation regarding Ashton, he was basically left to fend for himself by way of meeting expenses incurred in staying in London as well as touring the country advocating the cause.

At the time he had been sentenced to gaol in 1839, McDouall was left having to face up to the fact he had burnt through all existing assets he had to his name. How it must have added insult to injury when the prosecutor at his Chester trial inferred he had been out to make money from his Chartist involvement. Certainly, it presented a challenge to him now, emerging from his year in prison, to think how he could maintain his commitment to the cause. To his credit though, he managed to come up with inventive new ways to sustain him in his determination to go on playing a leading role in the movement. Needing to scrape a living together, McDouall tried to capitalise more directly on what he considered his three main areas of expertise, those of medicine, journalism and political involvement. At a later time, when he was to become even more desperate to find a way forward financially, he was to deny that he had profited very much from 'pills, pamphlets or politics'. [4]

For the time being though, he tried to revamp his approach to these three chosen spheres of activity of his.

First of all, pills… realising he was never going to be in one place long enough to conduct medical services in the same way he had done at his base in Ramsbottom, he looked for a different way of making money from his area of expertise. This is what led him to promote sales of a concoction called 'McDouall's Florida Medicine', (advertisements for which he placed in the Northern Star from as early as 19 September 1840) putting this commodity on sale for people attending his meetings. Given his original career intention to serve as a 'bona fide' doctor, an alternative view might have prevailed that he had been enticed into the quack medicine trade.

Secondly, pamphlets… he was soon to produce his own publication, printed in Manchester, entitled the 'Chartist and Republican Journal'. Apart from giving McDouall an added edge through being able to project his views more directly to a wider readership, the sales of this journal provided him with an extra, if far from substantial, source of economic livelihood. It is clear how much he revelled in the chance that owning a newspaper gave him to describe and comment on events, as in the case of McDouall's already quoted account of the parliamentary vote on the 1841 petition.

However, the majority of McDouall's column-space centred upon his persisting abhorrence of the Factory System and the degrading effect it had on all those working within it. His medical practice had 'provided him with tangible evidence of its horrors but his condemnation of the system was also tinctured with moral outrage'. [5]

This is evidenced in statements he made in the Chartist and Republican Journal such as the following: 'The factory system is rooted upon the worst passions of the human heart, avarice and ambition'. [6]

He condemned factories as 'hospitals of disease' where 'death presented itself under a hundred different forms'. [7]

With Wilberforce's lengthy campaign to abolish black slavery in the colonies fresh in the public mind, McDouall coined the phrase "White Slavery" to describe the yoke workers were still under in Britain's industrial north.

∞

The third part of the equation related to how he was going to play his hand on the political front. In this respect, he seemed more than ambitious to stay in the arena, as well as taking on new responsibility where opportunity might arise.

Indeed, his efforts to adapt to the new Chartist organisational structure proved highly successful. In two important electoral contests, first in 1841 and again the following year, he topped the poll both times. In June 1841, when the NCA had held elections for posts on its national executive committee, the vote-count showed the leading candidates in order: PM McDouall 3,795, J Leach 3,664, J Campbell 2,219, M Williams 2,045, G Binns 1,897, RK Philip 1,130. The next year too, McDouall was to win the highest number of votes, this time with an increased advantage over the same nearest rival, J Leach.

In 1841, a month after he had gained his tally of 3,795 votes, McDouall had travelled to Northampton to stand as Chartist candidate in the General Election of that year. His campaign was geared to the demands for political reform as contained in the People's Charter as well as opposition to the Poor Law. In an appeal to middle-class voters, he also approved the campaign for the repeal of the Corn Laws. A large congregation had gathered for what was the first stage of the electoral process, an 'unofficial' show of hands for everyone present to indicate which of the candidates they would vote for. At this initial stage of proceedings, he amassed an overwhelming number of endorsements over and above his Whig and Tory counterparts. But the rub of course was that the vast majority of his supporters were not eligible, under the conditions laid down by the 1832 Reform Act, to vote in the following stage of the process, namely the official poll.

If he had been successful, McDouall would have become the Chartist Movement's first MP. In the circumstances, he probably did well to garner 170 votes, despite the fact this total fell well below those gained by the two Whig candidates, 990 and 970 votes respectively, and the Tory candidate's total of 896. Even though his number of votes brought about the defeat of the Tory candidate, this was scant consolation. The sheer injustice of the whole business incensed McDouall. He knew all too well that if universal suffrage had been in place, he was bound to have been elected. Instead, he was baulked by the fact that the vast majority of his would-be supporters were disqualified from voting when it really counted. However, not allowing himself to be overly discouraged, his Northampton experience only reinforced him in his conviction that the political system, as it stood, was disgracefully elitist in the way it disqualified the working class from having any meaningful input into the process.

McDouall's lengthy campaign involvement in Northampton was probably the reason why his name did not show up as a resident of Ramsbottom in the National Census data recorded for the year 1841. Nor though was he recorded as being resident in Northampton. Although it was more than likely he would have been dwelling somewhere in the Northampton area at the time of the census, he somehow slipped through the net. [8]

∞

Since leaving Scotland to start his medical career in Ramsbottom, McDouall had very much committed himself to life south of the border. No doubt though, there would have been things about his home country he missed. Upon release from Chester prison, he had enjoyed the opportunity to re-visit by deciding to go up there to speak at Chartist rallies. Of course, there had been the added bonus of the marriage ceremony with Mary Ann in Glasgow.

1842 was destined to open badly with news coming to him that his father Andrew McDouall had passed away in Newton Stewart. No doubt coming as a severe shock to him, there are no details of the funeral arrangements, let alone Peter Murray's involvement in proceedings. In all events, it was inevitable he would have made it his business to pay due respect to his father, who had acted as such a strong influence on him in earlier life.

∞

On return to Ramsbottom, McDouall was actively in process of launching a fresh investigation into the activities of local factory-owners, William Grant and Brothers. Similar to the case he had delivered to the British Association in 1838, McDouall's evidence this time round though was to be given a much higher profile through being delivered to a Select Committee of Parliament.

Meanwhile, as stated earlier, William Grant had been in poor health from the late 1830s onwards. He was to die on 28 February 1842, aged 73, and 'was interred on the 5th of March, attended by a numerous procession of gentlemen from Manchester, Liverpool, and the neighbouring country. In passing their family monument, the funeral was joined by many hundreds of their workpeople and friends. The country and the village of Ramsbottom appeared one general scene of mourning from his hall (Springside) to the church (St. Andrew's) where he was laid in a vault, inside his own temple, which he had built and dedicated to the lord'.

Subsequently, a marble tablet, surmounted by a bust of the deceased, sited at the south side of the east window, was to be mounted on a wall in honour of William Grant. The tablet bore the inscription:

'Sacred

to

The Memory

of

WILLIAM GRANT of Springside, Esquire,

THE FOUNDER OF THIS CHURCH.

Born at Elchies, Morayshire, Scotland, on 15th April 1769,

Died at Springside on 28th February 1842.

Distinguished by vigour of understanding,

Spotless integrity of character, and true benevolence of heart,
He lived a benefactor to his species,
And died universally lamented'. [9]

As for McDouall's probable reaction on hearing the news, it is unlikely he would have chosen to be amongst the procession of mourners. For one thing, he would have considered it hypocritical. Nor, by the same token, was the circumstance of William Grant's death to deter him from continuing to prepare the case, involving the alleged misdeeds of the recently-departed local employer and Justice of the Peace that he was set on delivering to Parliament later in June.

∞

1842 was to prove a tempestuous year across the whole country and one which has been asserted to be 'the year in which more energy was hurled against the authorities than in any other of the 19th century'. [10]

Widespread disaffection came about as the direct consequence of an economic downturn. The so-called 'knife and fork' factor could be argued to have been pivotal in motivating working class people to sign up to Chartism as a means of making their protests evident to government. At the start of 1842, Chartist leaders as a whole had decided to submit another petition to Parliament. After all, a General Election had taken place in 1841 and it was argued a new composition of MPs might come to a different decision than that taken back in 1839.

The original intention had been to present the petition as early as possible after Parliament reassembled in February, but for various reasons the process did not reach fruition until much later. Finally, it was ready to be delivered to Parliament at the start of May, with organisers gaining added confidence from the fact the petition bore over three million people's signatures this time around, more than double the number three years earlier.

A strenuous case was argued, which a massive support-base could be seen to have signed up to, articulating longstanding grievances and translating them into a set of demands that it was fervently hoped Parliament would prove willing to accede to:

Parliament was not elected by the people, and acted for the benefit of the few;

- 900,000 people elected a government for 26,000,000;
- constituencies were unequal;
- universal manhood suffrage was a right;
- ancient laws declared there should be annual elections;
- property qualifications for MPs should be abolished;
- MPs should be paid;
- The Charter must become the law of the land.

Set alongside the above politically-based arguments, economic issues were also put forward for example:

- taxation was too high to be borne;
- there was too much disparity between workers' wages and the incomes of others;
- there might be violence if the distress and decline in wages continue;
- conditions, wages and hours in factories were appalling;
- agricultural labourers were paid starvation wages.

On the question of disparity of wages and incomes, a calculation was included, contrasting Queen Victoria's income per day of '£164, 17 shillings and 10 pence' with that of 'the producing millions'.

In more legislative terms, the petition:

- demanded the repeal of the Poor Law Amendment Act of 1834;

- objected to restrictions on the freedom of association;
- complained of the unconstitutional police force;
- objected to the use of the army in sensitive areas, as being unconstitutional;
- threatened revolution and violence if the grievances are not redressed;
- denounced the system of law which was partial.

∞

In the early hours of 2 May, detachments of Chartists, assembling in various parts of London, rendezvoused at Lincoln's Inn Fields, from which point the general procession marched to Parliament. The petition itself was mounted on a huge wooden frame, on the front of which was painted the precise figure: 3,317,702 (betokening the number of signatures) above the legend 'The Charter'. It must have presented a spectacular sight given that the petition, with that immense number of signatures, was said to be over six miles long. The sheer weight of it was sustained by a great bobbin-like frame mounted on poles, which required the efforts of thirty bearers to project forward. With everything in place, taking into account the petition itself and the huge number of Chartist supporters there on the day, the direct journey to Parliament now proceeded.

McDouall, on horseback, was chosen to be at the head of the Chartist procession. Next came the petition itself, then other leading members, headed by Feargus O'Connor, followed by a brass band. Upon reaching the House, the huge framework of the petition was found much too large to enter, and it had to be broken up with the various sections of it ending up strewn on the floor.

Meanwhile, Thomas Duncombe, MP for Finsbury, had agreed to put forward a motion of support to Parliament and he duly did so the next day on 3 May. As well, he put forward the argument that, with over three million people supporting it, Parliament should feel duty-bound to act upon the motion.

Despite the preliminary hullabaloo, the ensuing debate in the Commons turned out to be far from protracted. The long delay that had taken place in 1839, between handing in the petition and then waiting for the verdict, was not about to be repeated. Although there were some who spoke in favour of Duncombe's motion, the vast majority did not concur. The opinion expressed by Thomas Macaulay, MP for Edinburgh, was believed to have had a powerful influence on the day in swinging the argument against supporting the demands made in the petition. His chief objection was reserved for the demand for universal suffrage:

'I believe that universal suffrage would be fatal to all purposes for which Government exists, and for which aristocracies and all other things exist, and that it is utterly incompatible with the very existence of civilisation. I conceive that civilisation rests upon the security of property…I will assert that while property is insecure, it is not in the power of the finest soil, or of the moral or intellectual constitution of any country, to prevent the country sinking into barbarism'. [11]

As ever, the property issue played the predominant part in the thinking of the vast majority of MPs. The crunch for them was that a government elected by persons who had no property would give no security for those who had. Arising out of this central argument sprang other more emotive prognostications of what would happen to the country if the motion was passed. Distress, famine, and pestilence would ensue, and the resultant confusion would lead again to military despotism. England would fall from her high place among the nations, her glory and her prosperity would depart, leaving her an object of contempt'. [12]

There were still many who judged that the 1832 Reform Act, after extending the franchise to an additional number of middle-class voters, had already gone too far down the democratic road. Thus, in the minds of so many Conservative and Whig party MPs, the idea now of taking a further leap, involving giving the whole of the rest of the country the right to vote, with the vast majority of them owning no property at all, was plainly out of the question.

The result of the vote in the House, in the final count, echoed emphatically the outcome of that in 1839, with MPs in 1842 rejecting the petition put in front of them by 287 votes to 47. Chartist petitioners were not even able to claim they were getting 'nearer' in the process since the overall 'majority vote against' had escalated in the meantime from 189 in 1839 to 240 in 1842.

∞

While the line of reasoning was clear as to why so many MPs chose to reject this latest Chartist petition, it is interesting to take into account the more enlightened views of some of the minority of MPs who had voted in favour. One such was Benjamin Disraeli.

As well as an MP, Disraeli was a novelist. *Sybil or The Two Nations* was a novel of his which would be published in 1845. In it, the author portrays scenes showing the horrific conditions in which the working classes live. At one point in the book, the character Egremont comments: 'I was told that an impassable gulf divided the Rich and the Poor; I was told that the Privileged and the People formed Two Nations, governed by different laws, influenced by different manners, with no thoughts or sympathies in common; with an innate inability of mutual comprehension'.

If McDouall had been an exponent of this art-form rather than poetry, it was definitely the kind of novel he would have been proud to have written!

Disraeli, who had entered the House of Commons as a Conservative MP in 1837, had in fact taken it upon himself to visit the industrial north to examine what conditions were like. It is doubtful whether many of his fellow MPs, especially those like himself residing in the south of England, would ever have gone to the same lengths.

Returning to the plot of the novel, *Sybil* is set during the period 1837-1844. It portrays the working classes as underpaid and without the means to sustain a family. This is despite national wealth levels having risen significantly, due to increased production, trade and commerce. However it is shown how prosperity is concentrated in the hands of the upper classes: landed aristocracy, merchants and mill-owners. By contrast, Disraeli had indicated how, in the vast majority of cases, working people lived in abject poverty. Poor wages, long working hours, unsanitary working and living conditions, high infant mortality and short life expectancy, were factors which heightened the stigma of human degradation.

The bitter irony was that, while MPs such as Disraeli were supportive of reducing the 'gulf dividing the Rich and the Poor', the overwhelming majority of MPs were still definitely not.

∞

The 1842 rejection proved hard again for Chartists to take. As always seemed the case, there was anything but a unified response amongst leaders to this latest rejection. The 'blame game' was played out on different levels by different factions. There were those, and McDouall no doubt fell into this camp, who were becoming ever more disillusioned with the idea that presenting petitions was ever going to provide a recipe for success.

One extra 'ingredient' that had been added to the 1842 presentation was inclusion of economic and legislative elements in addition to the familiar political 'six points'. The original thinking had been that this gave recognition to the fact Chartism was more of an umbrella movement, ever needing to broaden its focus to appeal to a wider range of interests. In retrospect, there were those maintaining now that extending the range of 'demands' had only served to leave the movement fragmented, and needing to return to a concentration on achieving a more limited number of core objectives.

In the face of this latest setback, there were also many on the 'moral force' wing who felt it was misguided, or even plainly wrong-headed, to have written in the possible threat of applying force if Parliament were not to accede to the demands laid down in the petition. Running the risk of being interpreted as blackmail, post mortems had it that Parliament was likely to have rejected the petition on these grounds alone.

There was widespread anger and resentment among workers across the country at this latest rejection of a Chartist petition. This was not just directed against the Government but often also against their own leaders.

∞

As much as anyone else, McDouall was deeply disappointed by this latest setback. However, whilst many other leaders were left feeling deflated and bereft of purpose, McDouall was fortunate to have a quick, alternative means of occupying himself and keeping his spirits alive. This came in the form of making new accusations against the Grants, alleging this time that they were acting illegally through paying their workers in 'kind' as opposed to proper wages. In particular, McDouall sought to reveal how William Grant had over time exploited his role as a local magistrate to feather the nest of family business concerns.

The opportunity to present his case in London arose because Parliament had decided to set up a Select Committee, on the subject of 'Payment of Wages', giving it a remit to investigate the extent to which the terms of a certain piece of legislation, namely the Truck Act, were being contravened in different parts of the country.

By way of background, the Truck Act had originally been passed in 1831 with the aim of bringing an end to truck or so-called 'tommy' shops. In the earlier years of the Industrial Revolution, these types of shops were common in the vicinity of water-powered factories, likely to be situated in remote locations.

Often, in such shops, owned or leased out by factory-owners themselves, payment of wages had been 'in kind', usually in the form of tokens which could only be 'spent' or exchanged in the factory shop. It was argued that this practice had led to inflated high prices, poor quality food ('tommy rot') and a culture of 'tick', further enhancing the wealth of factory-owners at the expense of workers caught in a commercial trap which took ruthless advantage of their dependency.

The 1831 Act had recognised the need to break such dependency by insisting workers were paid their wages in proper money and not in any form of 'kind'. Now that the age of the old remotely-located factory centres was over and that the latest factories, powered by steam engines, tended to be built nearer to or within town-centres, Parliament had decided that there was no remaining justification or excuse for the old system to persist. However, despite the Truck Act having been passed, certain evidence had come to light in more recent times to suggest that various unscrupulous factory-owners around the country were circumventing the new legislation.

It was McDouall's contention that illegal activities, in contravention of the Act, were taking place within The Grants Arms in Ramsbottom, which was owned by the Grants and leased out to publican George Goodrick. McDouall was also mindful that William Grant had been involved as a Justice of the Peace in the issue of a licence to The Grants Arms. [13]

In the same way as he had travelled in 1838 to Newcastle to provide evidence, McDouall now found himself scheduled to testify to a Parliamentary Select Committee in London in June 1842.

∞

Constitutionally, the practice was that the House of Commons set up Select Committees (with cross-party representation of MPs and a group-size usually no more than about ten members), for the purpose of researching and investigating a particular matter of concern. The expectation was that the Select Committee would then issue a report for the consideration of Parliament as a whole.

A lot of importance was attached to the decision as to which MP was chosen to chair the group. Naturally, the stance taken by the Chair was likely to have a strong influence on how matters were conducted. McDouall must have been greatly heartened to learn that Lord Ashley had been chosen to chair this particular Select Committee. It would have been hard at this time to think of any MP with a stronger, more philanthropic outlook than Lord Ashley. Born in 1801, he had first become an MP in1826. Son of the Earl of Shaftesbury, he had received a public school/Oxbridge education. Given such a background, it might have been assumed he would inevitably have ended up towing the elitist line. However, despite his privileged upbringing, Lord Ashley was very much the exception to the general rule. Feeling genuine concern for the polarisation of the existing 'two nations', he had a broad enough insight into the scale of injustice operating across society to grasp what changes needed to be made to create fairer conditions for the working classes.

As principal instigator of the 1833 Factory Act, Lord Ashley had established his reputation for being a social reformer. Not content with just the passing of legislation though, he had in fact gone on to accuse the government in July 1837 of ignoring breaches of the 1833 Act. On this basis, he had moved the resolution to say that the House regretted the regulation of the working hours of children had been found to be unsatisfactory. Even though, ultimately, the resolution had been lost by 15 votes, he had vowed to continue fighting the cause.

Throughout his political career, Lord Ashley consistently applied his energies towards seeking to better the lives of the working classes. Hearing that Lord Ashley was chair of this Select Committee would have been music to McDouall's ears!

Others on the cross-party committee were:

Mr. Cobden
Mr. T. Duncombe
Mr. Ferrand
Mr. J. Fielden
Sir B. Hall
Lord Hillsborough
Viscount Jocelyn
Mr. Manners Sutton
Mr. C.P. Villiers. [14]

Four particular names, beside Lord Ashley's, would also have struck a very positive chord with McDouall. Not bad, given that the more radical type of MP was severely under-represented in Parliament in 1842. Amongst these four names, first and foremost would have been that of John Fielden. Born in 1784 and therefore a good few years older than Lord Ashley, he too had always shown himself an active supporter of the factory reform movement. Significantly, although a northern factory-owner himself, his experience of growing up in the town of Todmorden, on the border between Yorkshire and Lancashire, had led to him having a marked sympathy with the plight of the working class. Standing for parliamentary election relatively late in life, he had become an MP for Oldham in 1832. From that time onwards, he had strongly argued in Parliament not only on behalf of the broader factory reform movement but also for the repeal of the Poor Law Amendment Act.

Perhaps, equally encouraging on the face of it, McDouall would have known that Fielden had recently voted in favour of the Chartist petition. However, even if still sympathetic to the cause, he had since made clear he steadfastly remained on the 'moral force' side of the argument for reform as opposed to any other tactic being used.

Thomas Duncombe, radical MP for Finsbury in NE London, of all the members on the Select Committee list, was the one who had shown himself the strongest supporter of the Chartist cause to date. Two years running, last year and this, he had taken it upon himself to champion Chartist petitions to fellow MPs.

As well as Fielden and Duncombe, the names of Cobden and Villiers would also have resonated with McDouall. Charles Villiers had started out in office as a radical MP in 1835. Since then, his energies though had been devoted more in support of the Anti-Corn Law League than the Chartist cause.

Meanwhile, Richard Cobden, radical Liberal MP, had been the co-founder with John Bright of the Anti-Corn Law league in 1838. Born in 1804, he had become MP for Stockport in 1841. Representing English manufacturers, he would have had more in common with the views and values of the Grants. As a young man, similar to Daniel Grant, he had been a successful commercial traveller becoming co-owner of a highly profitable calico printing factory in Lancashire. Living in Manchester, it was the city with which he would always remain most closely associated.

∞

Overall, McDouall could have had little cause for complaint at the composition of this Select Committee. With good reason therefore to feel confident as to how his testimony might be received, McDouall must have keenly anticipated the opportunity to present his evidence at the Parliamentary Select Committee meeting scheduled for 17 June.

NOTES ON SOURCES

1. Northern Star 22 August 1840.
2. True Scotsman 19 September 1840
3. Chartist and Republican Journal: 2 June 1841
4. Northern Star 4 August 1849. N.B. This alliterative terminology of McDouall's was to inspire the title for P. Pickering and S. Roberts' article: *Pills, Pamphlets and Politics* - which appeared in the Manchester Region History Review (1997). With due acknowledgement to both McDouall and Pickering/Roberts, the author felt it only appropriate to give this chapter the same heading!
5. Owen R. Ashton and Paul A. Pickering, *Friends of the People*, p. 22.
6. McDouall's Chartist and Republican Journal: 3 April 1841.
7. Ibid 24 April 1841.
8. This matter is explored in intriguing detail by Andrew Todd in his article - *Radical Ramsbottom* in the RHS News Magazine No. 32 Summer 2007 pp. 10-14 - in which it is shown that James Parkinson (the Ramsbottom block-printer and staunch supporter of McDouall) was similarly unaccounted for in the 1841 census with records showing that his wife Alice had been alone on the census night at no. 72 Bolton Street. It is highly likely that Parkinson had gone to Northampton to campaign with McDouall.
9. William Hume Elliot, *The Story of the Cheeryble Grants* p. 206
10. Dorothy Thompson, *The Chartists* p. 295.
11. Mark Hovell, *The Chartist Movement* p. 255
12. Ibid p. 256.
13. The local circumstances leading up to McDouall's accusations are very well explained by Andrew Todd in his article, *George Goodrick, the Grants Arms and the Truck System* (RHS News Magazine No. 23: Spring 2002) pp. 11-20.
14. *Minutes of Evidence Taken before the Select Committee on Payment of Wages* in relation to the sitting of 17 June, 1842.

CHAPTER EIGHT

A Tale of Two Cities.

The proceedings which unfolded at the sitting of the Parliamentary Select Committee in London on 17 June 1842 are presented here on the basis of the 'minutes of evidence taken before the Select Committee on Payment of Wages'. [1]

(Note: the numbering system below (from 2048 onwards) – relating to the questions put to McDouall, together with his answers – was the one adopted in the formatted style of the minutes).

∞

The meeting starts with the Chairman, Lord Ashley, putting a series of preliminary, contextual questions to McDouall:

2048. (Chairman) 'Where do you reside?'
'In Lancashire, in the neighbourhood of Bury, at the village of Ramsbottom'
2049. 'Have you resided there any time?'
'I have resided there since 1835'.
2050. 'I believe you are a medical man?'
'Yes'.
2051. 'Have you many opportunities of mixing with the working classes?'
'Yes, many opportunities, at all seasons, and all hours, with all classes, both rich and poor in that neighbourhood'.

Note further: while various members of the Select Committee are quoted as asking questions during the course of the meeting, it has been assumed where no other name is cited, it is Lord Ashley, as Chairman, who is addressing McDouall.

2052. 'Does the system of paying wages in goods prevail in the district where you live?'
'Yes, in the majority of factories; at Ashton's factory it does not prevail; so that there is a contrast of the systems afforded betwixt the one side of the valley and the other'.

In common with the evidence McDouall had previously put forward at Newcastle, he again seems intent on establishing a contrast in terms of prevailing conditions in factories owned respectively by the Ashtons and the Grants.

2053. 'Have you observed the contrast of the systems?'
'Yes, I have observed a very great contrast, and have felt it myself; on one side of the valley, where the truck system is carried on (here it is clear that McDouall is referring to the Grants), my professional labours were not rewarded; on the other side of the valley (referring to the Ashtons as stated above in 2052), the remuneration was generally pretty regular'.

The above response from McDouall is not the only time during the meeting when he makes clear reference to what he sees as prejudicial treatment in the past towards himself from the Grants. It could easily have been construed that the doctor bore a grudge against the Grants on this account.

2054. 'Is it considered a great grievance to receive their wages in goods by the working classes?'
'Yes; it is a very great grievance, in many respects; it creates improvident habits among the people; it causes a reckless

spirit; they have no calculation among themselves as to the amount of goods they receive in payment of their wages, it causes them to procure whatever they may require without considering the result, consequently a great majority of them are debtors to the masters; besides, when they receive any money they squander it with a reckless spirit like schoolboys'.

2055. 'In what way are they generally paid?'

'They get whatever goods they require; food and clothing of all descriptions, the value being deducted on the pay-day'.

2056. 'Do you ever examine the quality of the goods?

'Yes, I have observed it'.

2057. 'What have you observed upon that subject?'

'That they always get the worst goods at the highest price'.

The focus of the meeting gradually shifts to workers' awareness of their rights under the 1831 Act.

2073. (Mr. Sutton) 'Do you think that the working classes are aware of the power they possess under the Act?'

'No, I do not think they are; and if they were, they are afraid to use it; they would be afraid to give me information, unless I promised to conceal the names'.

2074. (Mr. Ferrand) 'Have you known that lately?'

'Yes, more so than at any other time'.

2075. (Mr Villiers) 'They have known it to be against the law to pay in goods?'

'Yes'.

2076. 'They know that they can recover their wages if they sue the master?'

'Yes; but they also know that they are invariably discharged'.

McDouall is then asked a series of questions about why workers might be unwilling to come forward. Basically, his answer is that economic conditions are currently so hard with workers being laid off as a matter of course, let alone if they should complain about how they are paid their wages. Pressed for further detail as to how he has witnessed the truck system still operating, McDouall appears ready to give evidence of how the Grants were in effect running a truck shop in Nuttall.

Before he is able to describe this situation though, and as if by way of seeking clarification, a further pair of 'questions' are put to McDouall:

2160. 'You were speaking of the Messrs. Grants at Nuttall; do you mean Wm. Grant and Brothers of Ramsbottom?
    'Yes'.
2161. 'Wm. Grant has lately died?'
    'Yes'.

It is clear from the above that members of the Select Committee were aware that the widely-known industrialist had recently passed away. However, if anyone might have been thinking that this circumstance would alter or soften McDouall's stance, the nature of his monosyllabic answer suggests he has little intention of allowing it to modify what he has come prepared to say.

The questioning resumes in relation to conditions in Nuttall:

2162. 'Do they (the Grants) keep a shop themselves?'
    'No, not themselves, they are in too extensive a way of business, but they have a person employed that keeps a shop; there is only one shop allowed in the village, which contains 2,000 people; the shop does not belong to Mr. Grant, or any of his relations; an agent has the shop, there is no other in the neighbourhood, nor can there be within a considerable distance, for all the land belongs to Messrs. Grant'.
2163. 'Have the Messrs. Grant any interest in that shop?'

'I could not learn that, but I know the person who has the shop pays a very high rent'.

2164. 'What rent does he pay?'

'I cannot say; they would not inform me; that shop is better than a mile from the free shops and the whole land belonging to the Grants, no other person has a right to build upon it'.

2165. 'You do not know that they have an interest in the shop?'

'I am satisfied they have an interest in it, but it comes in the shape of rent; that is the way they have an interest'.

A set of questions then follow, aimed at eliciting details regarding exact amount of the 'very high rent'.

When McDouall seems only able to respond in general terms, a question is put to him which comes across though more as a statement of dissatisfaction at the lack of hard information being supplied:

2172. 'The amount of the rent is the proof we want that Messrs. Grant & Brothers have an interest in the business?'

At this point, McDouall appears quickly to change tack:

'I could prove it to you in another way; they have a very large inn in the village of Ramsbottom, and being magistrates, they take very good care not to license any other place'.

A series of questions and answers ensues, covering practices operating at this 'very large inn', namely the Grants Arms, which, without reiterating the circumstances, it will be remembered the Grants had opened as a hostelry in 1828. The committee does not pick up on the point McDouall makes that 'being magistrates, they take very good care not to license any other place' - an obvious reference to William Grant - but concentrates instead on a line of questioning about practices alleged to be taking place on the site of the Grants Arms.

2174. (Mr. Cobden) 'When you speak of their having an inn, do you mean that they own the building and carry on the business?'

'They own the building and the greater part of the village'.

2175. 'You do not know they have any interest in the public-house?'

'Yes, I am aware they have, because their wages are always paid at that public-house'.

2176. 'Are the wages all paid at that public-house?'

'Yes, for one set of workers principally; those employed in the dye-works are paid there, and the block printers...who receive notes from the book-keeper at the works, the landlord of the inn (McDouall refers here to George Goodrick) finds the change; they send up the whole of them under the plea that they cannot give them change; the men and boys bring up a note from the shop, and the publican pays them the difference on account'.

2177. 'You are speaking of the men employed in the dye-house?'

'Yes'.

2178. Not the block printers?'

'Yes, I speak more of them than the others'. (McDouall would have felt very confident on these grounds since James Parkinson, his friend in Ramsbottom and a block-printer himself, was likely to have supplied him with the relevant information).

2179. 'You say the block printers are paid in the public-house?'

'Yes, and 3d. is deducted from every man paid wages there.

2180. 'Is that the only proof that you have of their interest in the public-house?'

'Yes, and it is a very considerable interest; every man is compelled to spend 3d.'

RAMSBOTTOM'S REVOLUTIONARY DOCTOR

2181. (Mr Ferrand) 'He is compelled to spend it?'
>   'Yes; it is charged for the change, and the custom is compulsion'.
2182. 'He charges the 3d. for changing the tickets, and that they are obliged to spend in beer?'
>   'Yes; the little boys in the dye-house are paid there; I have seen them come down drunk.'

As will be recalled from previous mention, Goodrick was a trusted retainer of the Grants, having been butler to John Grant at Nuttall Hall, and it is clear he could have been relied upon to handle the firm's weekly wage bill, to make the appropriate deductions, and to use his control of the workers' wages illegally to boost beer consumption.

Not surprisingly, McDouall shows himself readily prepared to implicate the Grants in the practices operating at the Grants Arms.

2186. (Mr. Ferrand) 'Do you think the Messrs. Grants are aware of these men being paid there?'
>   'Yes, I am satisfied of it; if there was no other fact to reason upon, it would be evident that the landlord could not possibly have so large an amount of money in his own possession unless he had an order from the manufacturers upon the bank; I have travelled with him myself when he was bringing in a bag of silver; he goes to the town of Bury for it'.
2187. 'Is it Saturday evening they are paid?'
>   'Generally'
2188. 'How many of the men may have their wages paid there?'
>   'One hundred people; there may be more at times and less at others'.
2189. 'Three-pence is paid by each?'
>   'Yes'.
2190. 'Is it customary for the people to remain drinking?'
>   'Yes, I have known them remain there till they have exhausted

their credit and their money, and I have seen the little boys come down drunk'.

2191. 'Is the house improperly conducted?'

'No, the house is well conducted; but it is the love of the drink, and this unfair temptation which ruins the weak and injures the young'.

2192. 'What time is the house closed?'

'Twelve or one o'clock on Saturday night'.

In a later section of the meeting, questions tend to concentrate again, quite tellingly in a number of ways, on McDouall's experience as a medical practitioner in the Ramsbottom area.

2257. 'How do they (the workers) get medical assistance; do the masters provide it?'

'No'.

2258. 'Are there great complaints of that?'

'Yes; the working men complain that they cannot send for a medical man, and there is no chance of getting your account paid if you attend'.

2259. 'Is there any medical man attached to the factories employed by the masters?'

'Yes, but they are generally employed in signing certificates of age for young children; the surgeon signs these certificates, and the master favours him again'.

2260. 'Any medical man may sign these certificates?'

'Yes; but they always fix upon one individual, it is their interest to understand each other'.

2261. 'They do not allow any competition in that?'

'I never signed a certificate, though I had a large practice in the neighbourhood'.

2262. 'Does that arise from the interference of the masters?'

'Yes, and with the connivance of the inspectors'.

2263. 'They have appointed one medical man to the prejudice of others?'

'Yes'.

2264. (Mr. Sutton) 'Are you aware that the inspectors have appointed a medical man?'

'They have appointed Mr. Hutchinson of Ramsbottom'.

2265. 'Do you mean to say that the inspectors have appointed a medical man?'

'Yes, at least they sanction it'.

2266. 'It is only with the concurrence of the masters?'

'Yes, they have between them the appointment; the masters have an advantage in procuring from the surgeon the certificates for children, who appear to be tall and older than they really are'.

The latter response pointedly reveals he believes the Grants used the services of a doctor whom they could trust to rubber-stamp certificates providing false evidence of the ages of young workers. The inference is that the Grants wouldn't have wanted McDouall to carry out the same process because he would have been too honest and scrupulous in dealing with such matters.

The evidence gained from this section of the meeting confirmed that McDouall was far from happy about having been excluded from playing a proper medical role in their business.

∞

All in all, McDouall could not have denied having been given a fair hearing on the day.

However, looking at things from the point of view of the Grants, the investigation coming as it did little more than three months after the death of William, must have left a very sour taste in the mouth. Perhaps even more so in the light of all the eulogies that had been published on William's behalf in obituaries, most notably in the Manchester Guardian. The fact that this Select Committee was convening to examine alleged abuses of a Parliamentary Act, implicating William as both a factory-owner and local magistrate, would have cast a highly unwelcome blight on the life of a family in mourning.

Both parties, the Grants and McDouall, must have been keen to see what was going to come out of the report the Select Committee would be presenting to the full body of Parliament. For the time being, no-one had an exact idea of when that would be.

Absorbing as McDouall may have found the experience of testifying to the Select Committee meeting, events would quickly bring him down to earth again, knowing it was only a short interval before he was to be pitched back into the maelstrom of Chartist agitation.

∞

An ever-growing mood of despair had set in amongst workers during the summer months. Rapidly losing trust in the ability of national leaders, they began to feel they were better off taking action of their own on a more local basis.

By 1842, the economy had sunk to its lowest point. It was to be the year when 'the worst slump of the century occurred', with further devastating effect on wages and employment levels. [2]

With the depression hitting ever harder, employers had shown no compassion and actually imposed wage-cuts to offset their own profit-losses. Worker demands for restoration to previous pay-levels were ignored. Meanwhile, the devastating consequences of this sharp economic downturn on the lives of the work-force were plain to see for anyone who cared to look.

William Cooke Taylor, a journalist, made a tour of the Lancashire manufacturing districts in the summer of 1842. Everywhere he went, he reported disturbing scenes. For example, in Burnley, he came across 'groups of idlers...their faces haggard with famine and their eyes rolling with that fierce and uneasy expression which I have often observed in maniacs'.

Anticipating the scenario presented in Disraeli's novel *Sybil*, Cooke Taylor wrote that England had been divided into nations as distinct as the Normans and the Saxons, concluding that:

'In our wisdom we have improved on the proverb 'One half of the world does not know how the other half lives,' changing it into 'One half of the world does not care how the other half lives.' [3]

A wave of strikes, starting among Midland miners in the summer of 1842, spread to Lancashire and Yorkshire. Desperate crowds roamed from town to town demanding - and persuading with force on occasion – everyone they saw to stop work. In many textile mills, production halted abruptly when the steam engines were immobilised by the simple expedient of removing the plugs to the boilers. Thus, in Lancashire, the disturbances came to be called 'the Plug Plot Riots'.

In the Potteries, the properties of unpopular employers and magistrates were attacked and ransacked. McDouall was not exempt from getting caught up in the confrontations taking place during this troubled period. In August, he ended up involved in a fist-fight against Tory supporters in a wild brawl at Nottingham in the course of providing unsolicited help to the unsuccessful by-election campaign of the Quaker radical philanthropist and corn magnate Joseph Sturge. [4]

∞

In response to the increasingly chaotic state of disorder unravelling across the north of England, the authorities were intent on taking repressive action. Police and troops of soldiers attacked people who attended demonstrations. Many were arrested. In one incident in Preston, for example, soldiers had fired into a crowd, killing two and seriously wounding seven others. [5]

Such measures though only seemed to heighten the unrest. With a sense of nothing to lose, strike action became more prevalent with demands being put forward for an end to wage reductions, a repeal of anti-working class legislation and the enactment of the Charter.

The intense pressure the Government came under is evident from no less a source than the diaries of the then 23-year-old Queen Victoria who, within the safety of her Buckingham Palace residence, made a note on Saturday 13 August that:

'The accounts from Manchester are dreadful – such disturbances, as also in some other parts…'

'..found Sir Robert Peel (Prime Minister since 1841) and some of the other Ministers had come down for a Council, & I found a box from Sir Robert, in my room, in which he wrote that 3 magistrates had come to Town this morning giving an account of the bad state of things in Manchester, and expressing their anxiety that something should be done before the 16th inst, the anniversary of a great mob fight, which took place there in 1819, and some great explosion is dreaded for that day'.

What the young Queen was referring to as 'a great mob fight' was of course the Peterloo Massacre which had occurred on 16 August 1819.

The diary continues: 'We (presumably this meant herself and her husband prince Albert, whom she had married in 1840) saw Sir Robert Peel and he said that the whole thing had arisen from Anti-Corn Law people & Chartists having closed their Mills, telling the people they might play for a while, by which they immediately jumped at the conclusion they were to cease working. They marched in procession into Manchester, where they forced all the other Manufacturers to join them. It is the horrid system of agitation pursued by several Members, which is responsible for this serious agitation. They might be prosecuted if it could be brought home to them. It is proposed to send a Battalion of the Guards tonight, by rail, to Manchester'. [6]

The idea that the people had been told 'they might be able to play for a while' was a curious way of describing the situation. Despite the use of such phraseology, the seriousness of the situation facing the Government can be easily picked up from the above content of the Queen's diary. While sending 'a Battalion of the Guards' up by rail to the north was one way of contending with the immediate crisis, it would have been seen as little more than a stopgap measure.

Indeed, the scale of the on-going threat posed by Chartism was to force politicians into adopting longer-term methods of tackling the problem. Despite the expenses entailed, large-size barracks were constructed in quick time in Ashton, Bury and Preston, designed for cavalry regiments to be housed there in order to assist civil powers in maintaining law and order. When completed in 1843, the Ashton barracks had cost the then princely sum of £42,000 to build. It testified though to the Government's determination to stamp out rebellion in the north of the country.

∞

In the tumultuous atmosphere that was now threatening to get out of hand, McDouall felt it vital that the NCA should demonstrate a stronger degree of leadership than it had done to date. At one of its meetings in Manchester, taking place on 16 August, he moved a resolution committing the Association's membership to supporting strike action.

Beyond this though, he felt the NCA should make it a National Strike. The rationale was that whilst existing actions would go on receiving support from the Association, solidarity would be created through bringing in those parts of the country not yet involved. The strategy would entail remaining on strike until the Charter became law.

Reservations were expressed. For example, it is clear that some delegates, particularly those closer to Feargus O'Connor in outlook, suspected that the crisis was being fuelled by the Anti-Corn Law

League. From their point of view, it was feared that factory-owners had received encouragement from ACLL leaders to provoke a strike owing to the fact that over-production meant they now had too many goods in stock, and were looking for a means of not having to go on paying wages to workers in the meantime.

In these circumstances, it was argued that the NCA needed to be more careful before wading in too deep into matters that were more complicated than they appeared on the surface. However, despite such misgivings, conference overwhelmingly passed the motion. Delegates then empowered McDouall to write a manifesto which would articulate the rationale for bringing the whole working class together under one banner.

Mustering all his powers of rhetoric into the document, McDouall, in his appeal to 'the white slaves of England', proclaimed that:

'labour must no longer be the common prey of masters and rulers. Intelligence has beamed across the mind of the bondsman, and he has been convinced that all the wealth, comfort and produce, everything valuable, useful and elegant, have sprung from the palms of his hands; he feels that his back thinly clad, his children breadless, himself hopeless, his mind harassed, and his body punished, that undue riches, luxury and gorgeous plenty might be heaped on the places of the taskmasters, and flooded in the granaries of the oppressor. Nature, God and reason have condemned this inequality, and in the thunder of the people's voice it must perish altogether'. [7]

No-one in the movement could have been disappointed with the passionate nature of the rhetoric conveyed in McDouall's manifesto message. The question remained though as to how uniformly the plan of action would be carried out on the ground. The tactic of calling a general strike, with the condition built in that it should persist until demands were acceded to, very much depended on everyone sticking to the blueprint.

∞

However, from as early as 19 August, steady streams of workers in various parts of the country had begun returning to work on the back of local deals signed up to with factory-owners. By the start of September, only Lancashire and Cheshire were still strike-bound. The Manchester power loom weavers were the last to return to work on 26 September. McDouall and other Convention leaders, much as they kept on pressing the need for a sustained, collective approach, were powerless to stem the tide.

As far as achieving progress in establishing the 'six points' of Chartism, the National Strike of 1842 proved another failure. The commitment to the cause amongst its working class constituency had been seriously misjudged. However, on other more basic grounds, taking strike action had led to some success insofar as factory-owners had been coerced into restoring wage levels in the face of 'deals' signed up to with local work-forces.

Meanwhile, McDouall's impulsive decision to offer leadership to the struggle was to prove costly in personal terms. On two levels: firstly, many Chartists who looked for a scapegoat for the transparent failure of the so-called national strike evidently found one in him. According to the Northern Star, it was 'he who should shoulder the blame for the ensuing agony'. Editor O'Connor highlighted the Doctor's 'wild strain of recklessness'. [8]

Secondly, irrespective of the continuing internal wrangles being played out amongst Chartist leaders and membership, the authorities had meanwhile drawn up their own list of suspects. Not surprisingly, McDouall came out top of the 'wanted list' to hold to account for the insurgency that had threatened to break out across the country. After all, they knew it was he who had written both the manifesto and a letter to Chartists throughout the country, dispatched by the NCA conference in August. The warrant for his arrest, taken out on 19 August, shows they had been opening his correspondence for some time as well as keeping him under constant surveillance.

The 'wanted list' was to be a long one. In terms of seeking to arrest McDouall though, the authorities were to find him still more elusive than in 1839. However, in the vast majority of other cases, they were to be successful in their ploy of rounding up leaders, including the likes of O'Connor, and many more besides. Over fifty leading Chartists were arrested and committed for trial before being released on bail pending their cases being heard at Lancaster in March 1843. McDouall though was determined not to be amongst the number standing trial.

Gammage recounts how narrowly on several occasions McDouall survived arrest. This was despite there being a massive £100 reward on his head, as circulated on a poster, bearing the name of Sir Charles Shaw, the Chief Commissioner of the Manchester Police Service (dated 3 September), to be 'paid by the Government to any Person who shall give such Information as will lead to the Apprehension of the said Peter Murray McDouall, late of Ramsbottom, near Bury, Surgeon'.

Together with this general notification, the poster carried a physical description of the wanted person:

'He is about 27 years of age, stands about 5 ft. 6 in. high, inclined to be stout, has long dark hair, swarthy complexion, with high cheek bones, sharp black eyes, whiskers rather lighter than his hair; generally dresses in black; speaks quick with a Scotch accent'. [9]

∞

As Gammage reveals in his account of events at this time, 'the Doctor had many hair's breadth escapes from being pounced upon by the police'. [10]

On one particular occasion, Gammage describes when 'alighting at the Leeds station, he saw a policeman looking at him very earnestly; he walked boldly up to the man, and asked to be shown to an hotel, in which request the policeman obliged him. He invited his conductor into the house, called for brandy; but speedily contrived to give his official companion the slip. He stayed in Leeds, however, for a short time, but was so disguised that he completely eluded the vigilance of his pursuers'.

On another occasion, McDouall 'was going into Manchester, and called at a house on the way, where he saw the Northern Star portrait of himself hanging against the wall; he was dressed in a short dirty working jacket, and a cap, and his graceful locks were turned up out of sight. He asked his hostess how she dare have the portrait of such a man in her house. Her reply was encouraging. Pulling off his cap, his hair fell down, and the woman recognised him at once. In order with greater security to continue his journey, he prevailed on the woman, who was in her working dress, to accompany him; he could not, however, on this occasion escape the eye of one of the police whom they met on the road. The woman looking back after passing him, the policeman beckoned her to him, and advised her to get her companion out of the way as soon as she could, for the next policeman they met might not be so friendly'. As previously in Chester, McDouall seems to have evoked the sympathy of policemen who, despite being officers of the law, no doubt still appreciated what he was trying to do to support the cause of average working men like themselves.

By contrast, McDouall was not always so lucky in maintaining the support of certain of his fellow Chartist leaders during this period of trying to evade arrest. For example, the Northern Star not only sought to make him the scapegoat for the failure of the National Strike but also published accusations against him over the amount of 'expenses' he had claimed as a member of the NCA Executive.

Meanwhile, after much more dodging and weaving, McDouall had gradually found himself manoeuvring towards the south coast with a view to escaping to France. As Gammage further describes, 'the Doctor escaped to Brighton and went with a friend to the races at that town. Strange to say, they dropped by accident into the company of the Chief Constable, who told his friend that he had McDouall's description and portrait with him, and that he was on the look-out for him at that very moment'.

Far-fetched as such stories might sound, it did seem miraculous that McDouall somehow managed to escape arrest, especially at a time when there was a £100 bounty on his head. Ultimately in September 1842, he managed to reach France. Incidentally, he was not the only Chartist among his immediate circle of friends to have gone into exile. For example, William Aitken, his Ashton associate, had sailed off on a ship bound for the United States at this same time.

∞

For McDouall, the story of 1842 was indeed to turn out to be a 'Tale of Two Cities!'

Leading the procession in London that had taken the Chartist petition to Parliament in May and then testifying to the Select Committee in June, events had moved thereafter in such a way as to see him stranded in Paris by September.

However, his daring escape had been regarded in no kind light by many of his fellow Chartists, especially those who had been recently rounded up and committed for trial. Feargus O'Connor, for example, still went on blaming McDouall for the fact so many others had been arrested and led a campaign opposing any collections aimed at providing financial support for him in exile.

It is a matter of conjecture how McDouall's wife, Mary Ann, would have coped after her husband had bolted to the south coast to escape to France. He may have thought it better that he did not subject her to the perils of such a venture. It seems likely that, with having spent so much time in London serving as a Chartist delegate, he had contrived a rental accommodation somewhere in the city for his wife and children for as long as he might be away.

Meanwhile, having reached France, McDouall must have felt a pang of relief at having successfully accomplished his bid for freedom. However, in doing so, he had not only cut himself off from his wife and children but also any meaningful way of influencing what was happening in British politics.

Growing signs were to emerge of a general mellowing of official Chartist attitude towards McDouall and the situation facing him out of the country. In due course, he was to receive assistance from collections taken at several localities and even a donation from O'Connor himself. The occasional letter he sent to certain Chartist associates back in England made it clear though that despite this, he was finding it difficult it to make ends meet.

The situation he now found himself in did not seem to dampen his general ardour and appetite for work. Certainly, he was not to remain idle while on the Continent. It appears he had contacts he could call upon. Chiefly, there was Etienne Cabet, a Parisian whom McDouall had first met in London in 1839, at a time when the Frenchman had been in a spell of enforced exile of his own. The two men had much in common. Cabet, disillusioned by the reign of Louis-Philippe, after the so-called revolution of 1830, had soon afterwards started publishing a journal, 'Le Populaire' in Paris, which denounced the 'bourgeois' monarchy and instead championed the interests of the working classes. It was in these circumstances that the French Government had not only banned Le Populaire but also consigned Cabet to exile.

Spending the next few years in England, Cabet had spent a lot of time visiting the British Museum, studying the work of political thinkers. Having been allowed to return to France in late 1839, he had also been able to resume publication of Le Populaire. As well as this, he had embarked on what was to be an ambitious written work, *Voyage en Icarie*, in which he expounded his central political philosophy. As a recurring term running through the book, the author is held to have first coined the word 'communism'.

The background setting that Cabet created in his utopian novel was a futuristic one. Mythical Icarie was a democratically controlled state where families enjoyed happy lives. Free from want, life was full of healthful pursuits and minimal labour demands. Even the factories described in the novel were clean, brightly painted and well-lit. Given such a story-line, it is hardly surprising that McDouall, in addition to contributing to Le Populaire, was so impressed with the message coming out of the book that he undertook the translation of the book into English (with the title – *The Voyage of Icarus*) during his two years in France.

Not long after, Cabet had followed up with *Credo Communiste*, a book which was to gain cult status in the proletarian quarters of Paris in the early 1840s. The German writer Heinrich Heine, who had been living in Paris from 1831 onwards, noted the workers he came into contact with in the early 1840s were all describing themselves as Communists. To add further perspective, it is significant to note that these two works of Cabet's, introducing the concept of communism, both came out a good number of years before Karl Marx and Friedrich Engels were to project their *Communist Manifesto* on to the world stage in 1848.

∞

During the early 1840s, Paris had developed a reputation as a sanctuary for political exiles, covering a wide variety of nationalities. Karl Marx himself had been exiled from Germany in 1843 and then come to live in Paris. While it is believed that he and Engels had originally determined upon the title 'The Socialist Manifesto' for their 1848 publication, it appears they were influenced by Cabet's works to change the name of their pamphlet to *The Communist Manifesto*. They were swayed by the sense in which the word 'communist' conveyed the idea of revolutionary struggle better than 'socialist' did. At the same time, it established a clearer connection with the notion of common ownership and enjoyment.

Although the circle of political exiles living in Paris at this time would have been quite close-knit, it is a matter of speculation as to whether McDouall might have met up with Marx during the time he was in France. The opportunity was definitely there. In terms of an obvious link between the two, Marx would likely have been aware of McDouall's political background. After all, he was sufficiently aware of the general situation in England to have already contributed articles to Chartist newspapers and journals there.

Friedrich Engels, who ironically would have been in England during the two years McDouall was in France, had himself direct, first-hand experience of the Chartist movement and its struggle to improve the lives of the working class in England.

∞

Born in 1820 in Barmen, Rhine Province, Prussia (now Wuppertal, Germany), Engels' father was a wealthy factory-owner who owned large cotton-mills in Barmen and also, surprisingly, Salford in England. In the natural order of things, it would have been expected that eldest son Friedrich would follow in his father's footsteps. However, from the age of 18 onwards, he had started writing newspaper articles exposing the poor conditions endured by German factory-workers. In 1842, his parents had sent him to work in the Salford branch of the family business in the desperate hope that experience in England might somehow make him reconsider some of his radical opinions. Perhaps they just wanted him out of their hair in Germany!

Whatever the thinking, the scheme could not have backfired more severely. Almost straightaway, upon arriving in his new industrial setting, a defining moment came for him when he encountered Mary Burns, a passionate young Irish woman with radical ideas, who worked in the Engels factory. Very soon, Burns was to act as his guide through Manchester and Salford, in particular pointing him in the direction of the direst manifestations of the factory system. The bond between the two of them was destined to grow ever stronger.

Engels began penning accounts of experiences he was witnessing in Lancashire, bearing uncanny resemblance to him of cotton-mills in Germany. Ironically, one of the factory-owners whom he described meeting up with in his seminal book *The Condition of the Working Class in England* (published in 1845) was Thomas Ashton of Hyde.

Of course Thomas Ashton was also well known to McDouall. Despite some of the more pleasant things he was known to have said about the family's factory in Ramsbottom, it had been a different matter for McDouall when he had come across the Ashton factory in Hyde. Following evidence collected, he had produced a pamphlet with the ironically-intended title of *Hyde Paradise*. The picture of factory conditions that McDouall had put together was far from complimentary. Such had been Thomas Ashton's concern at what was projected that he offered to throw his factory open, ostensibly for visitors to discover the truth for themselves.

Taking up the opportunity, Engels had portrayed Ashton as a 'typical Liberal manufacturer who gave guided tours of his superb, admirably arranged building: he calls your attention to the lofty, airy rooms, the fine machinery, here and there a healthy-looking operative'. But Engels had made clear all was not as it appeared: 'the people hate the manufacturer, this they do not point out to you, because he is present; the factory school trained children to subordination and employees who read Chartist or Socialist papers and books were dismissed'. [11]

To be fair to the nature and extent of the research Engels had carried out in Hyde, he acknowledged how the Ashtons had some understandable reason to be hostile to radicalism after Samuel's son had been shot and killed in 1831.

Not finding it easy at first to gain a publishing outlet in England, Engels remembered having once met a publisher in Germany by the name of Karl Marx who, at this time in 1843, was in exile in Paris. Marx had been willing in 1844 to publish Engels' first economic work, *Outline of a Critique of Political Economy.*

In July 1845, Engels had brought Marx to Manchester. During a six-week stay, the two of them spent a considerable amount of time working together in Chetham's public library, a stone's throw away from the Ermen and Engels company office at 7, Southgate, situated behind what is now the House of Fraser department store on Deansgate. Apart from other articles Engels had published, his larger work *The Condition of the Working Class in England* was to come out in 1845, although at first only in German.

It is likely, especially bearing in mind the Hyde connection, that McDouall would at least have known of Engels and the research he had carried out, since it was in a similar style and direction as his own.

In due course, Engels was to leave England and return to Germany. Whatever further influence they might have sought to exert on their wayward son, Friedrich's parents must by now have despaired of him abandoning his radical views. On his way to Germany in 1844, he stopped in Paris to meet up with Marx, leaving Paris on 6 September.

∞

For the time being, the connections McDouall had in France would have kept him going at a time when he would have been feeling desperately out of touch with what was going on in his home land. One highly significant item of information though, which must have come to his notice, was the controversial outcome of the trials of leading Chartists that had finally been heard in court in March 1843. A total of 59 leading Chartists (including himself 'in absentia') had been put on trial at Lancaster assizes, in what was dubbed the 'monster indictment' with nine counts of inciting riots, risings, strikes and other forms of disorder.

The trials in Lancaster Castle had lasted eight days. Most surprisingly, breaking down the detail, the final outcome was that charges were dropped against seven men; nineteen others were acquitted and the rest, including McDouall, only had one or two charges against them upheld out of a possible nine. However, the sentencing side of the process had been adjourned.

Meanwhile, days, weeks and months had then slipped by without any further statement being made by the authorities. Could it have been a deliberate ploy to keep everyone, including McDouall, in an uncomfortable state of suspense?

Finally, towards the end of 1844, McDouall decided to take the risk of going back to England. Although still not sure of the fate awaiting him, he ended up returning home a free man. His sentence, in line with that of all others who had been tried at Lancaster, was destined never to be passed.

NOTES ON SOURCES

1. The first section of this chapter is based on evidence presented in the *Minutes of Evidence taken before the Select Committee on Payment of Wages*, relating to the meeting held on 17 June 1842.
2. Eric Hobsbawm, *Labouring Men* (Weidenfeld and Nicolson 1964) p. 74.
3. William Cooke Taylor, *Notes of a tour in the manufacturing districts of Lancashire* (Duncan and Malcolm: London 1842). As mentioned elsewhere, Taylor was a journalist hired by the Anti-Corn Law League to carry out research. I became familiar with his writings through reading the excellent book by Chris Aspin: *Lancashire, The First Industrial Society* (first edition published by the Helmshore Local History Society in 1969 and the revised edition Carnegie Publishing Ltd in 1995). This extract is quoted from p. 117 of the 1995 edition.
4. Thomas Cooper, *The Life of Thomas Cooper* (1872) pp. 156-61.
5. Mick Jenkins, *The General Strike of 1842* (Lawrence and Wishart 1980) pp.95-99
6. *Queen Victoria's Diaries* – Saturday 13 August 1842.
7. Peter Murray McDouall – *1842 Chartist Convention Manifesto*.
8. Northern Star: 20 September 1842.
9. Details taken from a notice of 3 September 1842, issued from the Town Hall, Manchester.
10. Gammage, *History* pp. 228-9.
11. Friedrich Engels, *The Condition of the Working Class in England*, in the Collected Works of Marx and Engels: Volume 4 (International Publishers: New York 1975) pp. 295-596.

CHAPTER NINE

The Murder of P.C. Bright

Returning in 1844, McDouall found the atmosphere very different to that which he remembered when last in the country.

Following the severe economic depression of 1842, there had been a notable upswing in fortunes. This had come as a blessing to all sections of society. With more plentiful employment opportunities and higher wage-levels, workers' spirits had picked up again. McDouall detected a lack of appetite for the political reform agenda that had brought workers flocking to the Chartist banner before.

He would also have seen a big difference in how the authorities seemed now to wish to capitalise on the stronger degree of economic prosperity. Interestingly, this involved taking what seemed a more tolerant view of past misdemeanours of Chartist leaders. The fact for example that sentences had not been handed out after the trials at Lancaster Castle in 1843 might have indicated a wish on their part to dispel any lingering sense of bitterness.

In other ways, it must also have seemed eerily different. Given the way he had been made a scapegoat for the failure of the national strike, McDouall would not have expected the same kind of rapturous greeting he had enjoyed upon his release from Chester gaol. In fact, there were no mass meetings taking place at all. Chartist support had shrunk to the point that no English branch possessed a total of more than 200 members now. Even within those branches that were still active, agendas concentrated on post mortems on what had gone wrong in the past as opposed to what the prospects might be for the future.

∞

There is no record of McDouall renewing residency in Ramsbottom on his return from France. Of course, the last serious involvement he had had there was in relation to the process of collecting evidence against the Grants in June 1842, which he had duly presented to the Select Committee in London. Despite having had a great many more matters on his mind since, McDouall would no doubt still have been interested to learn what was contained in the report stemming from the Committee's investigation.

On a similar account, the Grants too would presumably have wished to know the outcome of the inquiry. The blow to their pride would have been considerable if they had been impugned on the back of McDouall's testimony. For both surviving brothers, Daniel and John, it had been a bad time all-round in that first half of 1842. Daniel himself had been suffering from an attack of gout at the time, and the shock caused by his brother William's death had 'sent the ailment to his head'. [1]

The medical authorities had removed him immediately to his house in Mosley Street, Manchester, to be near his own doctor. It was said that for several days his life was despaired of. After a time, he had rallied and was able to return to Springside – not, however until a fair while after William's burial. All this with the investigation going on and McDouall's hostile testimony to be presented to Parliament in June.

∞

That meeting of the Select Committee had been more than two years ago now. However, no report had seen the light of day in the meantime. Perhaps the delay was due to not wanting to risk upsetting important manufacturers such as the Grants (particularly in the light of William's recent demise) if they should have been found culpable of breaking wage regulations. By the same token, the Committee would have been wary of whitewashing factory-owners should they have been found guilty of misdemeanours.

In fact, no report was ever published after the 1842 investigation. This outcome, or lack of one, emerges from the following Hansard archive content, discovered from 16 February 1854, in which it is stated that:

'From 1832 to 1842 complaints of evasion (of the said Truck Act) were frequent, and in the latter year a Select Committee was appointed to inquire into the truth of these alleged evils. The Committee did not report, but the existence of the evil was amply proved by the evidence adduced before them. In 1851 a deputation, composed of gentlemen from the localities in which the truck system prevailed, waited on the right hon. Baronet the Member for Morpeth (Sir G. Grey), then Secretary of State for the Home Department, with respect to these evasions of the Act, and in consequence a Commissioner was appointed to inquire into them'. [2]

If either the Grants or McDouall had been hanging on the outcome of the 1842 investigation, it is evident both parties could only have suffered disappointment. However, on the basis of the above Hansard content, it appears that McDouall would have had stronger reason to feel put out in the light of the above statement that 'the existence of the evil was amply proved by the evidence adduced before them'.

∞

Taking into account all the various other trials and tribulations McDouall had endured in the meantime, perhaps he might just have felt happy to be back in the country as a free man again. Even so, he appears to have found the general situation in England so dispiriting that, re-united with Mary Ann, they had set off to Scotland again. This move may well have had a nostalgic feel for them, recalling back in 1840 when they had travelled up there to get married. As well, it would still have been fresh in McDouall's mind how well received he had been in Scotland during his tour of speaking commitments on that occasion.

In the event though, this time round, McDouall could not deny encountering elements of disunity and dissension in Scotland. However, it perhaps wouldn't have entirely displeased him to learn that the cause of it was that many Scottish Chartists had a particular dislike for his rival Feargus O'Connor. He also picked up the message that they regarded the National Charter Association as an ineffective organisation failing to provide strong enough leadership, as well as not taking proper account of their own local issues.

McDouall listened closely to the idea put to him by many people he met that it might be better if the Scottish branch were to strike out as a separate entity. There was talk of starting up a newspaper, based in Glasgow. With his 'Chartist and Republican Journal' having gone out of business in late 1842, he would have welcomed the chance to renew activities as an editor again.

The upshot was McDouall, of course a native Scotsman himself, putting forward a recommendation that an independent Scottish Chartist Association should be created. Not surprisingly, although receiving enthusiastic support on home ground, the proposal did not go down well in England, where it was judged as a devious move on McDouall's part to build an alternative power-base for himself. It seemed particularly reprehensible to English onlookers such as O'Connor that, having been sent to Scotland under the auspices of the NCA, he should now be suggesting disaffiliation from the parent body. [3]

In response to such objections, McDouall posted his defence in the columns of the Northern Star:

'I simply suggested that, as all had apparently failed in Scotland, the best plan would be to appeal to her nationality'. [4]

However, McDouall's defence of his motives did not quell O'Connor's dissatisfaction. Indeed, this fresh bone of contention had the effect of opening up former grievances between the two.

McDouall's stock was at a low ebb generally with the NCA by this point in time. Having absented himself from the country for two years, his pugnacious approach now in Scotland was bound to raise hackles.

In a further attempt to curb his new ambitions, the NCA seemed intent on following up on the question of money it had granted him for his subsistence while living in France. This precipitated a quarrel between McDouall and James Leach, the NCA's spokesman in this matter. In a statement which could be construed as extended provocation on McDouall's part, he indulged himself in raking up old ashes of enmity by accusing Feargus O'Connor of lack of commitment in the part he had played in 1842 in relation to the call for a General Strike.

Despite the marked downturn in Chartist fortunes at this time, nothing seemed to quench the appetite for personality clashes with differences of opinion degenerating into angry recriminations. Picking up on what McDouall had accused him of, O'Connor directly entered the fray. Whatever the general pattern of disarray amongst Chartist leaders, O'Connor and McDouall seemed to have had one of the most vitriolic relationships of all. It is curious to try and imagine the two men locked together in argument, with such notable age, not to mention height, differences between the two of them. The imperious six feet plus O'Connor staring condescendingly down on the young, pint-sized McDouall! Yet some innate terrier-like quality about the latter, always capable of standing up for himself, suggests he would have given as good as he got.

Again, as with the feud that had developed in 1839 between McDouall and Stephens, each had their own bands of supporters. In a similar way, historians have tended to pick sides and support one leader against another. Whereas Gammage for example stood by McDouall, Hovell was most critical of him, commenting that 'his veracity and good faith are more than disputable, and his constant change of policy was at least as much due to self-interest as to instability. He was one of the least attractive as well as most violent of the Chartist champions'. [5]

With McDouall's stock so low amongst other leaders, who after all had stayed in the country to face their trials, it was not surprising that O'Connor easily won this immediate battle between them, leading to McDouall being compelled in the end to forfeit his association with the NCA.

Needless to say though, this did not stop him continuing to agitate further in ways that came naturally to him. For example, during the course of 1845, he was to publish a persuasive, well-argued pamphlet: *The Charter: What It Means! The Chartists: What They Want!* For the time being though, with the NCA and O'Connor in particular making their misgivings crystal clear to him, McDouall found himself removed from its official list of speakers. Instead, he was only able to make public addresses on occasions when he had received a local invitation to speak to an audience.

∞

Another development that McDouall could not have failed to notice on return was the way in which the Anti-Corn Law League had grown in stature in the meantime. Since being formed in 1839, its leaders Richard Cobden and John Bright had steadfastly refused to merge the ACLL with wider programmes of reform. Concentrating on the single objective of the repeal of the 1815 Corn Laws, the ACLL had a strong financial base to its organisation through the support of wealthy manufacturers such as the Grants and also significant parliamentary representation now as a result of five 'Leaguers', including Cobden in Stockport, having gained parliamentary seats in the 1841 General Election.

The ACLL, unlike Chartism, had consistently adhered to the policy of peaceful agitation. The moral argument for repeal was always the one pursued. To back the case with evidence, writers like

William Cooke Taylor had been funded to travel the manufacturing regions of northern England to research their cause in works such as his *Notes of a tour in the manufacturing districts of Lancashire* in 1842.

Meanwhile the level of support for other movements tended as always to go up or down dependent on the state of economic prosperity at the time. In 1844, fruitful harvests meant agitation was not so intense. However, the situation changed dramatically the following year with poor harvests and the 'Great Famine' of Ireland causing widespread starvation and unrest.

In 1846, a political crisis unfolded with Conservative Prime Minister Sir Robert Peel suddenly declaring himself in favour of repealing the Corn Laws. The trouble though for him was that he did not have the support of enough MPs in his own party, the vast majority representing the interests of protectionist landowners. However, on a historic occasion in Parliament on 15 May 1846, despite Peel having to rely to a great extent on the support of opposition Whig party MPs, the Corn Laws had finally been repealed with 327 votes being cast for the motion and 229 against, a majority in the end of 98.

With his own Conservative party divided down the middle and in complete disarray, Peel ended up resigning as Prime Minister. Lord John Russell, leader of the Whig party, took over the reins of government.

Peel's actions seemed difficult to fathom from a purely political point of view. On the face of things, it had to be seen as an altruistic step on his part to serve the best interests of the working class, as opposed to the rich landowning class that he had identified with during his political career to date. Yet it might have been that, coming from manufacturing stock himself, the first Prime Minister to have done so, that he also was seeking to help the cause of factory-owners who had from the very start supported the Anti-Corn Law League campaign. Perhaps ultimately a combination of the two factors at play.

Although he had to endure contempt from a broad swathe of his own party in Parliament for what he had done, the more consoling aspect for Peel was that, despite having to resign his leadership, he was hailed as a national hero in all other quarters.

∞

Meanwhile, the Chartist movement remained in the doldrums. As for McDouall, it was consoling to know that NCA hostility against him, and indeed that of O'Connor, had toned down. Hovell was to comment later that 'it is startling after all this to find that… O'Connor was welcoming McDouall back to the orthodox fold… There was no finality in the loves and hates of men of the calibre of O'Connor and McDouall'. This last statement was certainly portentous in relation to how subsequent Chartist events were due to unfold. [6]

Thankfully, for McDouall, there was renewed awareness of the strengths and qualities he could bring to the cause. In August 1846, an evident reconciliation seemed to have been struck which saw him becoming a NCA lecturer once more. Significantly, his fresh input received favourable mention in editions of the Northern Star.

However, the NCA's own chronic lack of finance was instrumental in limiting McDouall's activities on its behalf. No-one though could have accused him of being unwilling to support its programmes of action. One such was O'Connor's 'Land Plan'. Despite the fact that, in early 1847, McDouall had thought about starting up a medical practice in Oldham, this came to nothing and instead he decided to take up the option presented to him of becoming a lecturer for the newly-formed Chartist Land Company.

McDouall's knowledge of agriculture, combined with his powers of oratory, made him an eminently suitable advocate for this Chartist scheme. The basic premise behind O'Connor's plan was to entertain the prospect for industrial workers, who were otherwise abandoned to paying high rents in town slum-areas, to have the chance to make a small subscription, on a kind of lottery basis, to gain a smallholding in a more idyllic rural setting.

Commendable as O'Connor's Land Plan might have been in terms of intention, it was to be riddled with flaws in terms of practical operation. Even when a subscriber was successful, it would prove difficult to subsist, let alone compete, in the shadow of large landowners who were able to cut costs through employing the most up-to-date machinery and scientific farming methods. Worthy as it was as an attempt to revive older more harmonious methods of working, the plan was fraught with logistical problems.

McDouall no doubt appreciated all of the positive motives behind the scheme but may well have been attracted to it for other more grounded reasons. Firstly, it provided him with some kind of regular income for the time being. Secondly, it gave him a platform for expounding his views on matters of more general interest or concern to him. More than once though, his forceful manner of speaking was to land him in trouble with authority. For example, in late 1847, he was deemed to have overstepped the mark during a particular engagement in the Potteries. After the police had tried to break up a meeting of his in Newcastle-upon-Lyme, he confronted the local magistrates; on another occasion in Burslem he ended up being 'escorted by a posse of policemen out of the town'. [7]

∞

McDouall was to spend the early months of 1848 on a lecture tour in Scotland. His return to prominence was capped in the spring with his re-election to the executive of the NCA. In March 1848, he threw his hat into the political ring again, standing as a Chartist MP in a by-election in Carlisle. Perhaps he felt encouraged to do so after O'Connor had won one of two Nottingham seats in the 1847 general election. This had been by the spectacular margin of 1257 votes against the 893 given to Sir John Cam Hobhouse.

However, stepping in at short notice, McDouall was to endure very much the same experience again as had befallen him at Northampton. After a rousing speech at the hustings, he won the so-called nomination stage with an overwhelming show of hands in his favour. However, it was again his sad fate to win only a pitifully low number of votes, 55 in this instance, in the official poll.

With regard to the overall record of Chartists standing for Parliament, O'Connor was destined to be the movement's only successful candidate. Unfortunately though, his experience serving as an M.P. was to prove a desperately dispiriting one.

∞

With the country in the midst of another severe trade depression, breaking news hit the country in February 1848 of a fresh revolution in Paris. Unlike in 1830, when one monarch had been exchanged for another, this recent uprising had brought about an end to the monarchy and the creation of a Second French Republic. Together with the hunger and unemployment that was again now ravaging Britain, there was a burst of renewed Chartist agitation. Whatever hope the Government might have entertained that the Repeal of The Corn Laws in 1846 would curb working class unrest was to prove unfounded.

For radicals, the 1848 revolution in France was welcomed as a catalyst for uprisings in other countries. Although, in Britain, 1839 and 1842 had witnessed strong support for Chartism, the prospect was that 1848 would massively exceed those two previous years with regard to the potential ability of the movement to mount a threat to the existing order. At the same time as McDouall was campaigning in Carlisle, mass protests were breaking out in Manchester, Glasgow and Dublin. The Chartist Convention opened in London on 4 April. Although not a delegate, McDouall was involved in a debate taking place about the adoption of 'ulterior measures'. The conviction was held by militants like McDouall, weary with the tactic of petitions, that if the Charter could not be won by moral force, the feat must be accomplished by physical force. He was back to his original stance on matters.

The NCA as a whole, with O'Connor wielding major influence, did not however see it this way and instead decided in favour of holding a major demonstration, announced to take place on 10 April, to be held on Kennington Common in London. From there, a planned procession would carry a third petition to Parliament. Marches and demonstrations were also planned for that same day in Manchester and elsewhere.

For its part, the Government did everything possible by way of adopting counter measures. In anticipation of the announced march on Parliament, a statute was revived, dating back to the 17th century and the reign of King Charles II that forbade more than ten persons from presenting a petition in person. That was followed on 7 April by new legislation making certain seditious acts ('proposing to make war against the Queen, or seeking to intimidate or overawe both Houses of Parliament, or openly speaking or writing to that effect') felonies in Great Britain and Ireland, punishable by death or transportation. Even though the authorities had been informed that the Chartists were planning a peaceful demonstration, they sought to mount a large-scale display of force to confront the challenge. Enlisting thousands more special constables, London was turned into an armed camp.

With the atmosphere highly charged on the morning of 10 April, cabinet ministers waited to see what the Chartist reaction would be to the banning of its proposed march on Parliament. Faced by a large military force standing in its path, there was considerable tension in the air. O'Connor was to claim that over 300,000 people assembled on Kennington Common while the Government put the number at 15,000.

Meanwhile it seems some kind of 'deal' had been struck between O'Connor and Prime Minister Lord John Russell. The latter, apprehensive that a riot might break out, had arranged for 8,000 soldiers and as many as 150,000 special constables to be on duty that day. In return for allowing the meeting to take place at all, Russell appears to have asked O'Connor not to undertake a full-scale procession from the common to Parliament.

O'Connor, presiding over the meeting, strongly urged the crowd of people there to abandon the march on Parliament. His counsel was acted upon. The affair was a largely peaceful one throughout, finishing without incident. Later on in the evening, O'Connor presented the petition, having to hire three cabs to convey it to Parliament. His claim was that it contained 5,706,000 signatures, a significantly larger number than the last one submitted in 1842.

Unfortunately, when the signatures were officially counted by a staff of clerks, the total only amounted to 1,975,496, including apparent support from unlikely personages such as Queen Victoria, Prince Albert and the Duke of Wellington. Following on from this scrutiny, the document presented was viewed as little more than a laughing-stock by the vast majority of MPs and summarily rejected. Just as O'Connor's own reputation never recovered from this humiliation, the Chartist movement as a whole seemed yet again on the verge of collapse.

∞

In the aftermath of 10 April, McDouall, fuming at what had happened, once again became embroiled in conspiracy, chairing a secret insurrectionary committee in London. On 1 May, he attended a gathering of members of the National Assembly. There were reports of widespread anger about the latest rejection of a petition. Paramilitary organisations, collecting weapons and drilling, were quickly forming on a local basis. By no means for the first time, the question raised itself as to how action on the ground could be marshalled centrally by Chartist leaders.

Hard on the heels of the Kennington Common fiasco had been a motion put forward by London Chartists, under leader William Cuffay, to resort to more direct means. However, with government informants in ripe supply, this first local intervention had been instantly nipped in the bud. Illustrating the severity with which the authorities were prepared to deal with the emerging situation, Cuffay, as perceived ring-leader of the so-called 'Orange Tree' conspiracy, was summarily handed out a sentence of transportation to Australia with a minimal 21 years' penal service.

In an attempt to show Convention still had a central role to play, McDouall suggested creating an executive of five who would appoint ten commissioners for each of ten regions. Gaining support, the idea was taken up and put into practice. The duties of the commissioners would be to co-ordinate the activities of the district brigades. McDouall was chosen as one member of the executive of five. The others were Ernest Jones, who had been the foremost advocate of physical force at the Chartist Convention in April, James Leach, Samuel Kidd and John McRae from Scotland, where Chartists had already created a National Guard.

∞

In the meantime, Cabinet ministers, who had in April sought to dismiss the third petition as a pitiful fiasco, now began to become increasingly apprehensive again about the threat posed by Chartism. For example, Sir Charles Greville noted in his diary that 'during the past few weeks, there has been a great change for the worse among the people, an increasing spirit of discontent and disaffection, and many who on 10 April went out as special constables declare they would not do so again'. [8]

Added fuel to such fears came with news of a whole series of 'people's revolutions' taking place abroad, following on from the one in France that had led to the end of monarchy and the creation of the French Second Republic. Similar uprisings had taken place in many other parts of Europe including Germany, Italy and the Austrian Empire.

With revolution breaking out like wildfire on the continent during 1848, known in some countries as the Springtime of the Peoples or the Springtime of Nations, an added cause of anxiety for home authorities came from awareness of strong existing links between home-based activists and those of European nationality. Following his two year exile in France, McDouall could well have been cited as an example of someone who had contacts with foreign revolutionaries.

Clear evidence emerges at this point showing that Government representatives believed their country was in immediate danger from becoming infiltrated by influences from abroad. To give an example, the Earl of Arundel, who was Master of the Horse, expressed concern about the presence in the country of so many French and Germans with seditious and socialist designs. This statement was picked up on in the course of parliamentary debate by Lord Lansdowne, who, acknowledging the threat from foreign revolutionaries, pronounced: 'There are 40,000 or 50,000 persons not only prepared but desirous to seize the opportunity of taking part in overturning the government'. [9]

∞

As a member of the Chartist executive of five, McDouall saw it as an important part of his role not to let localised groups over-commit to action until proper preparations were in place. Uncharacteristically, this required him to play a calming influence in the weeks following on from the NCA meeting on the first of May. For example, he travelled to Bradford on 28 May to try to impress upon groups of workers, brandishing pikes and other assorted weapons, that the cause would be better served if they kept 'powder dry' until given the heads-up for being part of a co-ordinated country-wide call to arms.

Despite leaders striving to keep plans in-house, and away from the notice of government informers, news filtered through to authorities that 15 August had been decided upon as the date for a national uprising. Acting on this information, the forces of law and order now set about arresting ring-leaders, including McDouall, who had already been under close surveillance for some time.

Ashton-under-Lyne, his long-established stronghold, was also attracting government attention after its Chief Constable had reported to the Home Secretary on 16 June that there was a body of armed men in the town, called a 'National Guard', which was from 300 to 400 strong.

On 10 July, McDouall was in Ashton addressing a packed meeting held at the Charlestown Meeting Room at the local Stephensite chapel. The event had been advertised in advance with posters on walls around town with messages such as 'Equal Rights and Equal Laws' followed by: 'Hereditary Bondsmen, know ye not who must be free must strike the blow...' and 'Freedom's Battle once begun, bequeathed from bleeding sire to son, though often baffled, always won.' The Ashton constabulary no doubt had taken due notice!

However, with the aim of preventing potentially hostile witnesses attending the event, James Milligan, chief of Ashton's National Guard, took up post on the chapel door. After the meeting ended, a crowd had escorted McDouall to his sleeping quarters for the night at the Oddfellows Arms. In response to cheering from outside the public house, he took it upon himself to address the throng from an open window, which, given that it allowed several policemen to catch what the speaker had said, was to furnish the Chief Constable with evidence to arrest McDouall a week later for having made a seditious speech on this night of 10 July. He was committed to trial at Liverpool Quarter Sessions on 28 August.

As a further indication of the massive backing for McDouall in Ashton, the Town Hall Committee granted use of its large hall and anterooms for a great Tea Party and Dance which was held on Saturday 29 July for the purpose of raising funds for McDouall's trial defence.

When it became known that certain local policemen, PCs Pennington and Taylor had already supplied evidence against McDouall, Ashton's National Guard had marked them down for retribution.

On the night of 14 August, an extremely dark evening without moon or starlight, a small number of National Guard members confronted two policemen who were on patrol in the middle of town, happening to be PCs Taylor and Bright. It was Taylor the mob was after but he managed to escape. Then there was a loud report of a gun going off and PC Bright was lying dead in a gutter close to the Red Lion public house on Bentinck Street. [10]

There was an immense amount of remorse over the death of PC Bright, who had always been on good terms with the locals making up the National Guard. For certain, he had not been the intended victim on the night. Despite intensive enquiries though, it was never to be established for sure who had fired the shot that killed the constable.

At the trial, later to take place at the Liverpool Assizes in December 1848, several members of the Ashton National Guard were hauled up in court, facing a wide variety of charges and receiving severe sentences for varying degrees of involvement. However, the judge still seemed completely unsure by the end of the trial as to who had actually fired the shot that killed PC Bright. On the back of very slender evidence, a single statement made by one person on the basis of hearsay on the night, the judge finally arrived at the view it had been Joseph Radcliffe who was guilty of the murder of the policeman.

Clearly, despite the trial having thrown up little in the way of hard evidence, judge and jury had felt under significant pressure to identify a culprit. Hence, while dutifully following the judge's recommendation and returning a verdict of guilty against Radcliffe on the count of murder, the jury added a recommendation for mercy for the simple reason that members did not feel convinced at heart that it was he who was responsible for the death of PC Bright. Even the Judge himself, making his final address, admitted to not being fully satisfied that Radcliffe had fired the unfortunate shot, but nevertheless sentenced him to death.

On the back of all this uncertainty, it was no wonder that the Home Secretary was later prevailed upon by local MP Charles Hindley to commute the death sentence to four years imprisonment followed by banishment to Western Australia for life. Nevertheless, the original verdict of guilty of wilful murder was to remain on the statute book, perhaps as a counter to any notion that the matter had been dealt with too leniently.

∞

All this of course was anticipating events. Before the above sentencing, the trial of Peter Murray McDouall, albeit on the less serious charge of making a seditious speech, had duly taken place on 28 August 1848.

Notes on Sources

1. Hume Elliot, *The Story of the Cheeryble Brothers* p. 203.
2. *Hansard Report of a Debate on Payment of Wages* – Thursday 16 February 1854.
3. Alexander Wilson, *The Chartist Movement in Scotland* (Manchester University Press: 1970) pp. 209-10.
4. Northern Star: 9 December 1846
5. Hovell, *The Chartist Movement* p.263.
6. Ibid p. 264.
7. Northern Star: 31 July 1847.
8. *Greville Memoirs*, vol. 3, pp. 158-9.
9. *Hansard*, XCVIII, pp. 136-7.
10. A graphic account of events in Ashton on the night of 14 August 1848 is provided in an article by Herbert Davies, *A Shot in the Dark* pp. 16-28 - in *Victorian Ashton* - published by the Tameside Libraries and Arts Committee in 1974.

CHAPTER TEN

Serving Time at the

Kirkdale House of Correction

McDouall's trial at Liverpool took place on Monday 28 August, starting promptly at 9 a.m. [1]

Unlike at his trial in Chester in 1839, McDouall was not responsible on this occasion for conducting his own defence. Courtesy of funds raised at the Tea Party and Dance held at Ashton Town Hall on 29th July, he was able to afford a professional lawyer to act on his behalf.

The case was heard by Judge Cresswell. A one-time Conservative MP, he had resigned his post upon being offered a leading role in conducting the Northern Circuit. The advocate defending McDouall on the day was William Prowting Roberts, who had a record going back to the start of his legal career as a steadfast supporter of Chartism. His own general approach to fighting litigation battles could be summed up as: 'We resist every individual act of oppression; even in cases we were sure of losing.'

The charge against McDouall was constructed on seven separate counts. Making it as many as this seemed a saturation ploy to ensure he was convicted on at least one of the charges, even if it was likely to turn out many more. Basically though, the overall charge appeared to boil down to him having made a seditious speech on 10 July, 'in the presence of 500 persons', during the course of what was construed to be an unlawful assembly.

The initial question was put to the accused by Judge Cresswell: 'Are you guilty or not guilty?'

In the trial transcript, it is reported that the prisoner replied in a firm voice:

'Not guilty'.

The role of 'Attorney for the prosecution' was shared by 'Messrs Hall & Taylor' who started proceedings by supplying details to judge and jury as to what had happened on the evening of 10 July. They were informed of two meetings held in Ashton that evening, the first at 8 o'clock in a meeting room of the Charlestown chapel. Reference was made to the fact that entry was vetted and that it was not possible to quote what McDouall had said from 'the pulpit'. The fact though that some people, known to those on the door, had been refused admission was taken as a sign that seditious words would probably have been uttered by the speaker during the course of a meeting which lasted until '10 or 10.30 pm.'

It was the second meeting that the prosecution counsel concentrated on, taking place at The Oddfellows Arms, where McDouall was staying overnight. From the open window of his room, he was said to have addressed a large crowd standing below in the street. The following were the words attributed to McDouall:

'I advise you to organise and form yourselves into divisions, and sections, and practise the same drilling and manoeuvring as your enemy'.

The prosecution produced three witnesses. First was Robert Newton, Chief Constable of Ashton-under-Lyne, who stated he had tried to attend the first meeting at Charlestown but had been 'refused entrance by James Milligan'. He had though been present in the vicinity of the Oddfellows Arms and heard the above words spoken by the defendant.

Second witness for the prosecution was Henry Taylor, police officer in Ashton. Although it was not mentioned during the trial, this was the same policeman whose willingness to testify against McDouall had sparked fury amongst members of the local branch of the National Guard leading to the killing of PC Bright.

Third witness was George Dalgleish, Inspector of police for Ashton. These last two witnesses corroborated the evidence given by Chief Constable Newton.

Although the transcript reveals that 'Mr William Prowting Roberts was the Attorney for the defence', there is little record of him having actually spoken during the trial. This role appears to have been assigned to two 'counsels for the defence' namely, 'Mr Sergeant Wilkins and Mr Joseph Pollock'. No doubt they would have acted out Roberts' overall strategy on the day, usually a question of damage limitation.

It soon became clear they were left with only technicalities to work with. For example, it was said that McDouall had spoken for half an hour at the Oddfellows but that 'only selective parts of what he had said had been quoted in court'.

Significantly, the prosecutor chose to embark on a condemning personal observation about McDouall which was very similar in style and substance to the one made in his previous trial in Chester:

'He is a man of education; a man, I am told, of talent; a man possessed of considerable powers of eloquence, and likely to impose upon and impress the ignorant people to whom he was addressing himself'.

In the end, predictably, the defendant was declared guilty on all seven counts.

McDouall, who appeared not to have had chance to pass comment up to this point, was now asked if he had anything he wished to say. Seemingly rather late in the day, he said it was a pity he had not been allowed to have witnesses of his own. The judge brushed over this before moving on to pass sentence, amounting to two years imprisonment, adding that this would be at Kirkdale Gaol.

It is recorded that, in response to this apparent switch of detainment centre, McDouall said he had been in touch with certain members of prison staff at Kirkdale, which gave him cause for concern:

'From the confined state of the Kirkdale gaol, it will be impossible for my constitution'.

However, Judge Cresswell was not prepared to go into the question of McDouall's health condition, merely stating: 'You should have considered that before you made yourself amenable to the law. I cannot hear anything of that sort now'.

'The prisoner was then removed'.

∞

As crushing a blow as it must have seemed to McDouall, there might have been many in authority who felt he had been let off lightly with just a two-year sentence. Certainly a good many other sentences passed around this time, for similar offences, meted out severer punishments such as transportation to Australia.

For a man like McDouall, having experienced a custodial sentence before, perhaps it might have been assumed he was hardened, at least emotionally, to the prospect of the further stint of imprisonment lying ahead of him. Only now, it wasn't the same feeling for him at all compared to Chester in 1839. For one thing, he had then been a single man. By 1848, he also had to consider how his wife and their four children were going to cope in the circumstances of his enforced absence over two years. Additionally, by this later time, there was no longer any vestige of income or financial reserves to fall back on. Prior to his trial, McDouall had put it to Roberts:

'It is not for myself that I care about but what are the children to do?' [2]

His plight had been picked up in the columns of the Northern Star with particular reference to the sacrifices he had made in the Chartist cause:

'When he came among you he had good property in Scotland, a profession and a practice, which realised him several hundred pounds annually, besides a large sum of accumulated money in the bank. All of which has been spent long ago in the advocacy of the rights of the people'. [3]

In the meantime, in view of McDouall's further spell of incarceration, a fund was set up to enable Mrs McDouall to acquire a means of livelihood for herself and her four children in the form of a small business selling newspapers and general goods in a district of Liverpool.

∞

What exactly though was it about Kirkdale Gaol that, from McDouall's closing comment at trial, made it clear he was much more apprehensive about being consigned there than Lancaster prison?

If he had been sent to Lancaster, he would have faced conditions similar to those at Chester which did at least have some elements of being an open prison. Kirkdale was an entirely different proposition. Originally built in 1818 to serve as a county gaol for the southern division of Lancashire, its official title was Kirkdale County Gaol and House of Correction. Unusually, the prison had a built-in 'Panopticon' system which allowed prison officers to view inmates, at any time of day or night, without them knowing they were being watched. McDouall would have known in advance about this total infringement on an inmate's privacy.

Another 'feature' of this institution, built just a few miles outside Liverpool, was that public executions had become a common event taking place there. Such gruesome spectacles had the power to attract attendances of more than 50,000 people with railway companies putting on special train services to Kirkdale from other parts of Lancashire and the North West to gratify demand. Executions had taken place there since 1835 when James Barlow, of Bury, had been hanged for the crime of murdering his wife Priscilla.

Up until 1848, the site had witnessed eight more public hangings (religiously timed to take place on the stroke of noon) with that of William Adams, again for murder of wife, occurring in the same year as McDouall was installed into a cell there.

Accounts vary as to the full extent of the ordeal that McDouall was to be subjected to during his time in Kirkdale. On the one hand, he was not there for having committed a more blatant crime such as murder. On the other, there were elements of the media, for example newspapers like the Liverpool Journal, only too willing to express the view that it was a good thing that the distinction between so-called 'political prisoners' such as McDouall and 'common criminals' was becoming less blurred.

There can be no doubt though that McDouall found himself at the mercy of a prison-system that was designed for 'grinding men good'. For example, a fellow Chartist, John West, described the dankness of the cells they lived in:

'(they) are lofty with arched roofs, and a small aperture to admit air above the door, and an iron-girded window in front. There is no glass in this window, but wooden slides inside which close to. In the morning the bed clothing is quite wet, the blankets about our shoulders presenting the appearance of a field after driving rain or a heavy fall of dew'. [4]

It would appear that the 'small aperture' that admitted air above the door was something of a mixed blessing in that it would also have allowed rainfall to pour down into the cell.

During the further course of McDouall's stay at Kirkdale, another Chartist inmate, George White, reported that the doctor was 'suffering sorely in solitary confinement and not allowed to see, or speak to, any one'. [5]

It is not mentioned what had happened to bring about this particular type of punishment or how long it lasted. Despite the fact it was held that certain warders insulted Chartist inmates, deliberately worsening conditions, this does not appear to have happened, in the first instance at least, in McDouall's case.

Certainly, there is evidence to show he was given chance to make the best of the situation. For example, he found himself able on occasion to turn his hand to more constructive ways of occupying his time such as writing poetry or the odd paper on the subject of agricultural chemistry.

Having plenty of scope for reflection, McDouall's poetry homed in on nostalgia for the past, whilst at the same time ruing all the industrial developments that he saw as having changed the lives of ordinary people so much for the worse.

'Oh! for the days of the rattling loom', he wrote in a poem that was to be published in 1849:

'In the days of my father I lived by the loom

My song with my shuttle kept pace,

I knew not starvation nor poverty's gloom,

Strong was my arm and ruddy my face'. [6]

This extract is taken from a piece entitled *A Poetical Petition to Queen Victoria*. In choosing such a title, it would no doubt have been playing on his mind that if three politically-based petitions had failed to have the desired impact, what was the harm in putting forward a poetically-based one?

Despite these occasional, creative ways of spending his time, the core experience he was to endure at Kirkdale took a heavy toll on McDouall. By May 1849, for example, Mary Ann was letting it be known by way of public appeal, probably having picked up similar information to that George White had, that her husband's health was failing as a result of 'twenty-three hours close confinement out of twenty-four'. [7]

As well as occasionally writing poetry, McDouall also seems to have written articles, one or two of which appeared in the Northern Star. However, these were not to have the spiky, political edge to them of previous times.

All correspondence, out-going and incoming, would presumably have been vetted by the prison authorities and acted upon if containing any hint of seditious content. Existing conditions were bad enough without an inmate risking getting into deeper water by penning reckless remarks. If McDouall had though fallen foul of the authorities in such a way, perhaps bringing on a spell of solitary confinement, he could hardly have been surprised at the outcome.

Evidence from the missives of McDouall's, that we have to go on, presents a very different picture though. Rather than making any overt political statements, he dwells instead on how personally oppressed he feels in the throes of his second spell of prison sentence.

For example, in August 1849, he states feelingly:

'I have suffered imprisonment twice - exile once - and endured the privations of a wandering, houseless lecturer, during a period of ten years. I have sacrificed time that might have been more profitably employed – health, that ought to have reaped a better reward – and talent, that might have secured a far higher and lasting remuneration'.

By way of conclusion, he states: 'I have claims upon the Chartist body, and upon the working men, of more than a common character'.

In this same article, he is at pains to illustrate how strong his commitment has been but at enormous cost to both himself and his family, going on to say he had 'spared neither property, person, nor family. I have been unjust to myself, negligent to my children, and forgetful of my private duties, that I might concentrate all upon the people'. [8]

Reading the above, the prison authorities might well have interpreted the despondent tone of the message as conveying a spirit almost of penitence. In the depths of despair as McDouall must often have been in at this point, such a take might not have been far wide of the mark. The fight seemed very much to have gone out of him. At the heart of all his anguish, he was haunted day and night by the torment he felt from picking up reports of how his wife and children were at starvation's door. Even worse, the sense of powerlessness from knowing he was barely half way through his prison sentence at this point.

∞

Despite the modest assistance from Chartist victim funds mentioned earlier, Mary Ann and the young children were indeed suffering increasingly severe hardship by this time. Any original hope that Mary Ann might have been able to create an independent income, for herself and the children, through the small business selling newspapers and general goods in Liverpool, had proved ill-founded. The enterprise, basically depending on the custom of the 1,600 employees, who worked at the nearby Berry's foundry, came unstuck as a result of a protracted industrial dispute which left the local area a virtual ghost-town.

In June 1850, with McDouall's release from prison imminent, someone called James Sedlif recorded visiting his wife only to discover that her eldest child, a 10-year old girl, had just died. He described how 'the mother sat, the large tears dropping on the dead body, not a sixpence in the house or a mouthful of food'. [9]

∞

When it came to McDouall's eventual release and meeting up again with Mary Ann, the shared grief over the recent death of their eldest child, must have been insufferable for the two of them.

For his part, McDouall would have tortured himself knowing that this tragic loss happened at a time, however close it had been to his date of release, when he had still been locked away and unable to do anything to intervene. Emerging from prison this time around, with a feeling totally different to that of breaking free of Chester a decade earlier, McDouall now stated he was removing himself from the political arena to confine himself to 'the pen and the lancet'.

Aided by his long-time friend and fellow Chartist, William Aitken, McDouall went about setting up a medical practice in Ashton-under-Lyne, collecting in subscriptions from the community intended to assist in the purchase of necessary medical equipment. However, something obdurate in McDouall's character made it impossible to retire from politics altogether. As Adams was later to put it, 'agitation had unfitted him for a regular life'. [10]

Within weeks of release, by way of illustrating that the old fire hadn't entirely died out, he addressed a large Chartist gathering at Blackstone Edge on the Pennine moors letting the assembled crowd know, in no uncertain terms, that:

'he had been imprisoned for two years in a small cell, yet he treated the authors of it with the most sovereign contempt'. [11]

He had also embarked on editing a newspaper called 'McDouall's Manchester Journal'. Its pages include a curious blend of issues that he sought to pursue. Taking special account of what he was able to offer in his capacity as a qualified doctor, the back page of the Journal contained a promise to provide 'MEDICAL ADVICE' for a seemingly modest fee of two shillings and sixpence: 'the requisite prescriptions can be given, either privately, or in a printed form in the Journal'. [12]

Meanwhile, the Northern Star, suffering declining circulation, recommended 'McDouall's Manchester Journal' to its readers, albeit rather sarcastically hoping that it would enjoy more success than his previous journalistic endeavour. Unfortunately for McDouall's continuing hopes as an editor, such apparent optimism was to prove ill-founded with the demise of the Journal after only a handful of editions.

As for hopes of resuming his role as a medical practitioner, the attempt to establish a practice with the support of William Aitken in Ashton fell short of fruition. To what extent this was due to lack of necessary funding or else insufficient commitment on McDouall's part is difficult to say.

Nevertheless in 1852, not letting recent disappointments unduly upset him, McDouall felt emboldened to take the step of standing again for the NCA Executive. Buoyed up no doubt by memories of how well he had fared in such ballots before - ending up top of the poll two years running back in 1841 and 1842 - the result this time brought him crashing down to earth, not only failing to gain election but only managing a paltry 51 votes in the process.

The ignominious defeat he suffered in June 1852, together with the fact the Chartist cause in Britain stood at this stage at such a low ebb, was bound to concentrate McDouall's mind. Searching for another way forward, was it so surprising that McDouall came to believe that the future interests of he and Mary Ann, together with their children, would be better served by taking off on a journey to a place of greater promise.

The circumstances were very different but one can't help thinking the McDouall family's motivations at this point echoed the feelings the Grants had had, deciding to move lock, stock and barrel from Scotland to England back in 1783.

Setting out to Australia, though, was a rather more hazardous proposition.

Notes on Sources

1. The account, in this chapter, of McDouall's trial at Liverpool Court, taking place on Monday, 28 August 1848, is based on a transcript of proceedings: courtesy of Tameside Local Studies Archive Centre in Ashton-under-Lyne.
2. Northern Star: 22 July 1848.
3. Ibid: 29 June 1848.
4. Ibid: 17 March 1849.
5. George White in *The Harney Papers* p. 90.
6. Northern Star 27 October 1849.
7. Ibid: 5 May 1849.
8. Ibid: 4 August 1849.
9. Reynolds Weekly Newspaper 9 June 1850
10. Adams, *Memoirs* p. 212.
11. Ibid p. 212.
12. McDouall's Manchester Journal 20 July 1850.

CHAPTER ELEVEN

Life and Death in Australia

McDouall's plan to go to Australia might indeed have seemed a strange one.

Since the first batch of convicts had been conveyed to Botany Bay in January 1788, the common notion was that people only ended up there if they had been sentenced to transportation, the equivalent of being handed a one-way ticket to oblivion.

During the Chartist period of agitation from 1838 onwards, men like John Frost, Zephaniah Williams, William Jones and William Cuffay had been dumped in penal colonies like Van Diemen's Land, now known as Tasmania. By whatever margin McDouall had escaped a similar sentence in the past, it would have seemed self-defeating to many that he was now choosing to consign himself and his family to the antipodes. Even if exercising free will, the decision might still have been thought to smack of desperation.

In truth though, the idea of going there had become a much different and almost exciting proposition by the time, on 19 June 1852, the story first broke in the papers that McDouall had announced his imminent departure to Australia. [1]

Disillusioned with life in Britain, he would also have had strong reason to feel a positive impulse as to what the future held for himself and his family through going out there.

By 1852, emigrating to the Southern Continent had grown in appeal to the extent it had almost become a cult thing to do for people seeking a freer life. This change of perspective was one which was often picked up in the Chartist press in Britain. For example, in the same edition as McDouall had first announced he was going to

Australia, it was stated in the editorial that 'no workman need starve at home while comfort and independence await him in Australia'. [2]

'The future Australian republic', continued the editorial, 'will be a refuge and a home for those of our workers in the cause of the people, whose souls shall yearn for liberty, should they ever be... compelled to abandon in despair the people of the British islands'. [3]

Meanwhile, the last mention of McDouall in England records him, late in November 1852, having engaged in Chartist debates taking place in Manchester. Sometime, not too long after this, it is believed the McDouall family must have set off on their 12,000-mile journey.

∞

In the space of only a few years, Australia had suddenly become a beacon of hope as a land of freedom and opportunity. One man who had played a large part in this change of perception had been John Dunmore Lang. Born in Scotland in 1799, he was a Presbyterian minister who had in 1823 followed his brother out to New South Wales. Inspired by the Chartist movement and more recently by the 1848 revolution in France, Lang had been the first prominent advocate of Australian republicanism. Alongside Henry Parkes and James Wilshire, he had founded the Australian League, putting forward visionary and radical ideas such as colonial federation, the establishment of a fully democratic government and the creation of an Australian republic.

After Lang had started up a campaign aimed at achieving a federal republic, England's Northern Star (then still in operation) had anticipated a quick resolution in favour of the motion: 'Let people at home make common cause with their brethren in Australia, and the downfall of aristocratic domination is certain. If Englishmen in America and Australia can conduct their affairs well, wisely and prosperously under a Republican form of government, why not at home?' [4]

Following advice put forward in a commissioned 1839 report by Lord Durham, the British government had embarked on a project intended to grant the settler colonies what was called 'responsible government'. Perhaps there had been a fear that, if local freedoms weren't made allowance for, what had happened in America might replicate itself in Australia.

A notable political breakthrough was perceived to have been achieved with the UK Parliament's passing of the Australian Colonies Government Act of 1850, setting up legislative councils to govern the various states, with the majority of these councils made up of elected members.

Whilst the Northern Star fairly put the question why such allowance could not be given to Englishmen 'at home', the painful truth was that, whilst being prepared to make certain concessions of this nature in far-away Australia, the UK Parliament wasn't suddenly about to risk making rash changes in the way the mother country, at the heart of Empire, was itself governed.

As well as pursuing his political aims, Lang had been long conscious of the need to boost Australia's work-force to make the country's economy viable. To this end, during previous years, he had organised several immigration schemes. Invariably, though, these had come unstuck on the back of a combination of factors: his own lack of organisational acumen together with a basic dearth of incentive in the job market in the first place.

However, the discovery of gold changed all that. The announcement of one Edward Hargreaves that he had discovered gold at a place called Guyong near Bathurst in New South Wales seemed to solve the migrant problem in one fell swoop, with potential prospectors swarming to the continent from all points of the compass like moths to a candle.

The whole economy was instantly galvanised into life. Not only this but there was also a sense in which radical and democratic aspirations, feeding off the discovery of gold, provided an extra dimension to the escalating bid for national independence.

∞

In such circumstances, it was hardly surprising that many Chartists, like McDouall, might have felt this was the place to go. After all, there was little hope that the movement's aims were about to be fulfilled in Britain any time soon. Rather than ploughing on in depressingly familiar territory, why not switch location to where conditions seemed so much more favourable all round?

However, in all but Chartist papers, it was undoubtedly the lure of gold that dominated the attention of the broader public. The sensational story broke in much the same way as the Californian gold strike had done two or three years before.

News had first reached Britain in September 1851 at the height of the popularity of the Great Exhibition, staged in the 'Crystal Palace' in Hyde Park London. At a time when the government was intent on commemorating the achievements of the British Empire, both past and present, it may have seemed somewhat incongruous that news of this nature, from such a faraway location, was bombarding the headlines and motivating ever-increasing numbers of its citizens to depart for distant shores.

∞

Embarking on a sea voyage to Australia was however by no means a light undertaking and certainly not for the faint-hearted...

On a journey that might take as long as four months, life at sea was uncomfortable and hazardous, particularly for passengers who travelled cheaply in 'steerage' (the lowest deck and below the water-line). Storms were common in the Southern Ocean, but were not the only danger. Hygiene was poor at the best of times and worse in bad weather. The order to 'batten down the hatches' meant passengers on the lowest deck were confined without ventilation or light in conditions that were highly conducive to the spread of disease.

The use of candles or oil lanterns was restricted and sometimes forbidden. Cramped conditions with timber and straw mattresses meant a fire could spread very quickly. Any disaster at sea left little hope of rescue. Few sailors could swim, let alone passengers, and life-boat provision was usually well below that necessary to accommodate numbers on board in an emergency.

Regardless though of the difficulties and dangers, Australia had become a most popular destination for free settlers by the start of the 1850s. With the discovery of gold in 1851 and a booming economy, increasing numbers of people were now intent on taking their chances travelling out there.

In the 1850s, in an effort to speed up the journey, ships' captains had adopted the new 'Great Circle' route. Passing far south of the Cape of Good Hope, they sought the 'Roaring Forties', the strong prevailing winds that blew from west to east between 40 and 50 degrees south.

This route involved taking great risks from drifting icebergs and wild seas generated by frequent storms. Approaching Australia itself required exceptional navigational skills, as the slightest error could bring on disaster. The large number of ships that were lost when navigating the narrow path between King Island and southern Victoria led to the West Coast of Victoria becoming known as Shipwreck Coast.

∞

The exact logistics of McDouall's journey to Australia still remain, in many respects, shrouded in mystery. First of all, despite it being clear he had announced his intention of going to Australia in the Star of Freedom, there has been speculation as to whether he did actually set off after all! However, in his 'reminiscences',

Gammage raised and rejected any notion of McDouall having not in fact emigrated, as opposed to ending up dying in poverty in Manchester. [5]

On another tangent, it has been put forward that he had sailed to Australia aboard a ship called 'The President' but that the vessel, in tune with a past pattern of disasters taking place on the final approach, was shipwrecked and, despite his wife and children being saved, McDouall himself drowned off the Australian coast. [6]

Later research carried out, based on an examination of the evidence behind the theory of shipwreck and drowning has rejected this alternative explanation as to how McDouall's life ended. For one thing, the findings from this research established that, during the period in question, The President was permanently anchored in Hobson's Bay, Melbourne, where it served as a prison hulk, in other words, a ship that was still afloat but incapable now of going out to sea. [7]

Of course, the effect of these findings, even though proving he couldn't have sailed on the said particular ship, wouldn't on the face of it entirely rule out the possibility that he might have sailed on another vessel which did end up being shipwrecked.

The search for the existence of a death certificate - to account for how McDouall died - has drawn a blank with there being no record made of McDouall's death in any of the official notices of the Australian colonies covering the period in question from 1852 onwards. [8]

Taking all of this into account, ultimately the most reliable testimony to go by is that provided later by Mary Ann herself who said that her husband had died from illness shortly after they had arrived. [9]

Scant as the reference is to exact circumstances such as place and precise cause of death, it is highly probable that, one way and another, McDouall would not have been in the best state of health at the start of 1854. This was in the aftermath of a debilitating two-year period of confinement in the 'House of Correction' at

Kirkdale gaol and then, relatively soon after, a four month long sea experience in the gruelling conditions described above.

Keeping faith with the basic statement made by Mary Ann - there is no reason to believe she had any reason other than to tell the plain truth of the matter - it is still relevant to speculate on exactly how long they were in Australia before he died. The only clue given is that his death happened 'shortly after they had arrived'.

There is no evidence to show where he and his family may have been living after arrival. Nor has any mention been found of McDouall's name in connection with any events taking place in Australia from the probable time he would have arrived in the country in 1853 or early the next year. Ironically though, the year 1854 was to prove a major landmark in the country's history. This was certainly so in relation to matters McDouall deeply cared about, such as gains made towards winning political enfranchisement for working-class members of society.

∞

Two Chartists, who arrived in Australia in the early 1850s, for whom there is record of involvement in such action, are Charles Nicholls and his brother Henry, four years younger. In 1853, they had moved from New South Wales to the state of Victoria, recently constituted under the Australian Colonies Government Act of 1850. Although NSW was where gold had first been located on the continent, what was called the 'Finger of God' had swiftly moved in the direction of Victoria with much more substantial findings, making it the new centre of the goldmining industry.

The motivation behind the brothers' move in 1853 to Melbourne, capital of Victoria, had been to join George Black, another Chartist, in editing the anti-government 'Diggers' Advocate', a paper designed to support the rights of workers in the gold industry who were being exploited by their bosses – a situation akin to the Factory System 'modus operandi' back in England.

Following the demise of the newspaper in September 1854, the brothers were approached by goldminers to come and join them on the ground in the protests they were conducting against employers regarding working conditions.

The so-called 'Eureka rebellion' (named after the Eureka goldfield in Victoria), taking place in November 1854, occurred after the protest movement had rapidly transformed itself into a serious political force. This took shape as the Ballarat Reform League, which campaigned on the same points as embraced by the original British 'Charter' of 1838. It is clear that several leading members of the League were Chartists. Among the thousands of miners, many of them recent immigrants, there must have been large numbers who had been involved in the Chartist cause in Britain in earlier years.

Scornful of compromise, the authorities' response was to dismiss all attempts at negotiation or conciliation and to despatch troops to deal with the situation. An armed rising was crushed with relative ease. In a confrontation taking place on 3 December 1854, 5 troopers lost their lives compared to 22 miners (14 directly and 8 later from wounds received). This final encounter took place after the troops carried out an assault on a hastily-erected stockade within which the protesters made a last stand under their banner, a flag showing the Southern Cross. Although many survivors amongst the fighting miners were at first charged with treason, none were convicted of the offence.

The manner in which the miners had been treated throughout was seen as rank injustice. A hostile groundswell of opinion rose up in intensity against the authorities in following weeks that led to democratic reforms being conceded to during the course of 1855. The Nicholls brothers survived the stockade episode unscathed but took it upon themselves to campaign actively for improvements in miners' working conditions and also the political aims of the Reform movement.

The legacy of the Eureka rebellion was to serve as a catalyst for a process of fundamental changes in governance over the next few years that caused Chartist demands to succeed in coming to fruition in Australia long before they did in Britain.

∞

As for McDouall, it seems likely that his death, which Mary Ann stated had happened through illness, would have occurred before the Eureka rebellion took place and the democratic breakthroughs that followed.

Whilst he would obviously have regretted not having chance to actively participate in such giant steps forward being taken, he perhaps might have felt some consolation, however transiently, from being able to experience some satisfaction just from having been on the continent at the time. However ill, he must still though have picked up on the exciting sensation of being in a 'new world' scenario, in much the same way as his grandfather would have experienced from being present in America in the heady atmosphere of the late 18th century.

Added to that, he must have felt a strong bond of camaraderie from being a member of the large contingent of Chartists who, almost in the spirit of a crusade, had braved it together on the long, arduous journey to arrive in a land of promising, new opportunity.

Ultimately, although McDouall wasn't to live to see the progress achieved, significant further victories were to be won in the struggle to achieve democracy, not only in Australia, but later in his own country of birth.

The precise manner of McDouall's death is still shrouded in mystery. Investigating the various different possibilities involves the picking and unpicking of fragments of largely circumstantial evidence. The fact that no fuller picture emerges, apart from the summative testimony provided by Mary Ann, is problematic in itself but somehow also symptomatic in other ways of the difficulty in uncovering the full detail underlying quite a few episodes in the life of the 'mysterious Doctor McDouall'.

∞

Meanwhile, Mary Ann, bereft of her husband and stranded in the helpless circumstances she now found herself in, opted not to stay in Australia a moment longer than necessary. She and her five children (aged between 12 and two) survived and in due course returned to England.

However, life ahead of them back home was to prove anything but easy. At first, they lived as parish paupers in Liverpool before a subscription among McDouall's old Chartist associates helped her set up a stationery business in Nottingham. [10]

In the late 1850s, times still remained hard and unrelenting. It can only be hoped that Mary Ann managed to scrape together a sufficient income from her small business to support herself and her children through the no doubt hard times that lay ahead of them.

Notes on Sources

1. Star of Freedom: 19 June 1852.
2. Ibid.
3. Ibid.
4. Northern Star: 14 September 1850.
5. W.H. Mael (ed.), Robert Gammage: *Reminiscences of a Chartist* (1983) pp. 23-4.
6. Ray Challinor, *Peter Murray McDouall and Physical Force Chartism* (1981) p. 24.
7. P. Pickering and S.Roberts, *Pills, Pamphlets and Politics: The Career of Peter Murray McDouall (1814-54)* footnote 67 of article.
8. Ibid.
9. Quoted in People's Paper: 9 August 1856.
10. Ibid.

CHAPTER TWELVE

Postscript

Had McDouall lived longer, it is interesting to speculate whether he would have ventured to write an autobiography.

One Chartist friend of his from Ashton days who did was William Aitken.

Aitken said he embarked on *Remembrances and Struggles of a Working Man for Bread and Liberty* partly by way of an attempt to understand his own life, but also because he believed that, if the lives of the ruling class were deemed worthy of recording, then so were those of working people. In the second line of his book, he puts it like this:

'All things have a history; and the struggles of many of the working men of this country, if placed upon paper, would read as well, and be as interesting as the lives of many a coronetted lord'. [1]

As one might expect, the autobiography starts with Aitken's early years. He gives his date of birth as 'about the year 1814' which makes him an almost exact contemporary of McDouall's. He too was born in Scotland: in Dunbar, about thirty miles east of Edinburgh on the North Sea coast. At a very young age, his family had moved to Ireland because that was where his father, a sergeant-major, was stationed.

When Aitken was eleven, his father retired from the army and the family had moved to the north-west of England. One of his sisters had married a Lancashire man. Aitken came to work in a cotton factory. On the back of this arduous experience, he was, like so many others, to become drawn into the folds of Chartism. Educating himself independently, he started to earn a living as a schoolmaster.

Sadly, the autobiography only takes the reader as far as 1840 when Aitken was about 26 years of age. As far as providing us with a first-hand account of McDouall's early involvement in Ashton, it is though valuable in establishing important detail regarding for example his arrest and trial in 1839.

The reason for the autobiography being unfinished was due to the fact that, on 27 September 1869, Aitken committed suicide. Suffering at the time from a severe bout of depression, which rendered him incapable of continuing his work as a schoolmaster, he cut his throat with a razor in the bedroom of his Ashton house.

The exact set of circumstances leading to him taking this course of action remains complicated to piece together in retrospect. As well as the factors mentioned above, views he had recently adopted towards America seem to have made Aitken prey to added mental turmoil.

The 'New World' had always had a certain fascination for him. Recalling how he had departed the country to go to America at the same time as McDouall had gone into exile in France, Aitken's experience abroad was to stay vividly in mind, prompting him to have written *A Journey up the Mississippi* in 1845 in memory of his stay at a Mormon settlement in Nauvoo, Illinois.

Returning to England two years later, events of 1848, mainly those in Ashton which culminated in the murder of PC Bright, made Aitken opposed to taking militant action from then on. Instead, he had adopted a more measured stance in the direction of Liberalism which for him involved entering into alliance with middle-class radicals.

Back to the subject of America, he found latest developments there extremely troubling to absorb. Fundamental differences in outlook were to precipitate the outbreak of a Civil War in the early 1860s between Northern and Southern states. What followed not only had a deeply disturbing effect on his own psyche but also impacted much more broadly on the cotton industry as a whole in Lancashire.

Following the outbreak of the American Civil War in 1861, Northern forces had blockaded Southern ports, which in effect also cut off Lancashire's vital raw cotton supply at root. Between 1861 and 1864, the resultant level of unemployment in Ashton had reached an unprecedented sixty percent of the work-force.

The stance Aitken had maintained throughout the 1860s was to support the South, on the basis of safeguarding NW England's cotton industry. This was despite the fact that the North, under Abraham Lincoln, had put its own political emphasis on an anti-slavery stance that more liberal-minded citizens of Ashton put greater store by as an issue. Favouring the cause of local trade, Aitken's conscience must have been torn by the thought he was at the same time going against other beliefs he cherished strongly, namely, liberty and the rights of man.

It is clear to see how, beset by a whole number of anxieties, Aitken found himself driven to an overwhelming state of despair, leading him in 1869 to take his life. On the day of Aitken's funeral, it was reported that thousands 'thronged the streets'. [2]

Aitken's autobiography was serialised in The Ashton News in 1869 over five weeks from September to October. A further aspect of Aitken's writing, which no doubt would have had resonance with McDouall, was a propensity to translate his thoughts and feelings into poetic form.

While those who had attended his funeral might have chosen to see Aitken's life as one devoted to a cause that would eventually reap dividends, his own more pessimistic inner doubts are revealed in his poetry. The following extract from *The Captive's Dream*, might be seen as epitomising the sense in which the poet may have become resigned to viewing the task of achieving 'equality' for the working man as an illusory goal:

'Equality her banner wav'd
And from destruction Britain sav'd;

Despotic laws were known no more,
And freedom rang from shore to shore.
And rich and poor in union join'd,
And all their energies combin'd,
That freedom's start might brightly beam –
I woke, alas! 'twas but a dream. *3*

∞

McDouall might well have kept in correspondence with Etienne Cabet after returning from his two-year exile in France. However, it is highly unlikely that the two would have met up in person again.

By 1847, only a year in fact before the 1848 Revolution, Cabet appears to have given up on the notion of reforming French society from within. At the head of a group of followers, he had set sail from Le Havre on 3 February 1848 for New Orleans, Louisiana with a view to developing an Icarian community on American land. Perhaps he may have taken with him a copy of McDouall's English translation of his seminal work, *Voyage en Icarie*, to display to Americans.

Upon landing, the party trekked to the Red River valley in Texas. Unfortunately, the hoped-for Utopia was not realised and, ravaged by disease, a third of the group had returned to France. Ironically, those remaining then re-routed to the same location, Nauvoo Illinois, where Aitken had stayed in the mid-1840s. By this point, with the Mormons having vacated the site in 1849, Cabet's Icarians settled there. By 1855, the community had expanded to 500 and seemed to be flourishing.

In 1851, Cabet had to return to France to settle charges of fraud brought against him by his previous followers who had returned back there from Texas. Acquitted of these charges, Cabet had returned to Nauvoo in 1852 but found the character of the community had changed in his absence, departing from Icarian principles. Trying to restore his authority must have been stressful.

Suffering a stroke in November 1856, he died soon after. However, the community he had founded was to survive a good while further before finally disbanding in 1898.

∞

Meanwhile, Friedrich Engels was destined to enjoy much greater success in promoting his radical ideas. In the 1848 'year of revolution', he and Karl Marx had collaborated to produce their *Communist Manifesto* which had ended with the passage which was to become world-famous: 'Let the ruling classes tremble at a communistic revolution. The proletariat have nothing to lose but their chains. They have a world to win. Working men of All Countries, Unite!' [4]

In 1849, Engels had returned from the continent back to England, re-entering the Manchester company in which his father still retained a vested interest. He did so in order to earn money which would then be spent financially supporting Marx at a time when the latter was labouring on with his major work *Das Kapital*. The irony could not have been lost on them that the fruits of Engels' continuing involvement in 'big business', however reluctantly pursued, subsidised his colleague's scathing critique of the capitalist system.

Unlike his first period in England in 1843, Engels now found himself under police surveillance and had to be careful how he maintained correspondence with Marx, as well as supplying articles to Chartist journals. Despite all this, Engels rose to become a partner in the firm in 1864. Throughout, he had continued in the same unmarried relationship with the fiery Irish factory-worker, Mary Burns, whom he had first met twenty years ago.

In 1863, Mary died suddenly of a heart disease, after which he became similarly close to Mary's younger sister, Lydia ('Lizzie'). Aged 50, Engels retired in order to focus on his studies. With Lizzie accompanying him, he moved to London, where they lived openly as a couple, eventually going through with a marriage ceremony only hours before Lizzie's death on 12 September 1878.

Engels had moved to London to be able to work more closely with Marx after his close colleague had taken up residence there. Combing through all the countries in the world that might be deemed most ready to embrace Communism, the two had identified Russia as the most likely seed-bed for revolution. Eventually, Marx died in 1883 and Engels twelve years later in 1895. It would be twenty-two years afterwards that the Communist Russian Revolution broke out in 1917.

∞

Whilst it cannot be denied that Chartist agitators such as McDouall had doggedly pursued the cause from beginning to end of his life, many others like Dr Matthew Fletcher and the Rev. Joseph Rayner Stephens had, as shown earlier in the text, recoiled fairly quickly in 1839 from further involvement. This must have come as a disappointment to McDouall, given that these were the two men most influential in signing him up to the movement in the first place.

After 1839, Fletcher appears to have returned to Bury and settled back into the life of a GP, having nothing more to do with Chartism. In the 1851 census, he is shown as lodging with a foundry owner by the name of Thomas Parkinson. In those of 1861 and 1871, the widowed Dr Fletcher is living in Bury with his four grown-up daughters and a servant.

Although abandoning Chartism, he still maintained a major interest in the cause of factory reform, his name cropping up in local newspapers on a regular basis giving evidence in cases where workers had been injured. His name also appeared on a list of prominent local supporters of reform at a time when the 1867 Act was making its way through Parliament.

Fletcher was a man from a secure middle-class background. Although remaining radical in outlook, he seems to have come to a snap decision in 1839 not to risk having to make the large-scale sacrifices (for example as endured by McDouall) which he must have feared lay ahead of him if he had continued being a Chartist.

In terms of longevity, Dr Matthew Fletcher undoubtedly benefitted, living on to the age of 82.

∞

The Rev Joseph Rayner Stephens, after his release from Chester prison, had returned to Ashton, where he conducted services at a chapel on Wellington Road. In 1852, he moved to nearby Stalybridge and continued to preach until 1875.

As mentioned previously, a great deal of acrimony had stacked up between Stephens and McDouall during their time in Chester prison. Incidentally, no objective evidence was ever unearthed to show that the Reverend was guilty of sexual improprieties with the sister of fellow-Chartist James Bronterre O'Brien, a charge that had been levelled against him by the Doctor.

Stephens had married Elizabeth in 1835, who died in 1852; secondly, in 1857, Susanna, and had children from both marriages. Although claiming to the end not to hold allegiance to any particular party or cause, he went on employing his oratorical skills from the pulpit to argue in support of issues he felt passionate about. He was also a member of the Stalybridge school board. His contribution to education was to be acknowledged, very much later in July 2017, when a secondary school was named after him, the Rayner Stephens High School in Dukinfield. Troubled by gout and bronchitis in his last years, he too reached an advanced age, into his mid-70s, dying in 1879.

Of all those associated with the movement, Stephens' role was the most enigmatic. Speaking out forcibly at Chartist meetings in the early years, he didn't seem to appreciate how far it would get him into trouble with the authorities. Then claiming he had never at any point been a Chartist only made him seem a renegade to many others within the cause. Perhaps, he had thought he could go on indulging his passion for making public speeches with impunity. However, after being arrested by Bow Street Runner, Henry Goddard, and suffering imprisonment, he scaled down his radical involvement considerably on release.

McDouall, Fletcher and Stephens, each in their own different ways, exemplify a significant point once made that 'the middle-class Radical and the idealist intellectual were forced to take sides between the "two nations". [5]

Whereas all three started out with full commitment to championing the rights of the poorer "nation", Fletcher and Stephens quite soon lost their appetite for fighting the cause when realising what they were up against in terms of taking on the authorities.

∞

From the time of Stephens' arrest onwards, the scale of punishment handed out to those publicly espousing the cause of Chartism escalated dramatically. While the argument raged on in Chartist circles between 'moral force' and 'physical force' wings as to the most effective tactics to pursue, it was clear how the authorities viewed the situation. Not unexpectedly, the most severe sentences were reserved for those either advocating an armed uprising or indeed, like John Frost, actually conducting one.

Following the Newport Rising of 1840, Frost and two other colleagues were granted the dubious distinction of being the last men in Britain to have the sentence of 'hanged, drawn and quartered' passed on them. In due course, the sentence was commuted to transportation for life to Van Diemen's Land, or Tasmania as it is known nowadays.

Soon after his arrival at this far-off point, which was to remain a penal colony until 1853, Frost had done himself no favours when overheard to make disparaging remarks about the Colonial Secretary at the time, Lord John Russell. For this blasphemy, he was assigned two years' hard labour.

As a result of work on his behalf by radical MP Thomas Duncombe, a pardon was granted in 1854 for Frost, allowing him to return to Britain. However, Frost did not take up the option. Instead, he ventured to America where he undertook an extensive tour of the country, organised by Chartist lawyer WP Roberts, lecturing on the unfairness of the British system of government.

In 1856, Frost eventually sailed back to Britain, continuing to advocate reform. To say he had been condemned to die so many decades earlier, it was to prove something of a miracle of longevity on his part too that he survived to the age of 93.

∞

Another Chartist who suffered the perils of 'transportation for life' to Australia for his misdemeanours was William Cuffay. It may be remembered that in 1848 he was tried in London at the same time as McDouall was in Lancaster. Although circumstances of cases were bound to vary, the latter was said by many to have been fortunate to receive only a two-year custodial sentence on home soil. McDouall's treatment apart, what additional prejudices might have been operating at the time leading to Cuffay being sentenced to lifelong transportation?

William Cuffay was born in London in 1788. His father had been a slave in the West Indies island of St Kitts but had become a free man and served as a ship's cook. He had eventually settled in London marrying a white woman. Son William had grown up with a spinal deformity but proved himself proficient enough to become a registered tailor. He had become politically active after a strike taking place in 1834. By 1839, he had become a Chartist.

From that year on, he had become active as a leader of a section of London-based Chartists. 'Punch (magazine) lampooned him savagely, and The Times regularly referred to his group as 'the Black man and his Party'. [6]

In 1848, as described earlier in the text, Cuffay's radical faction had become involved in plans for a show of 'physical force' as a protest against O'Connor's decision to call off the planned mass procession from Kennington Common to Parliament to present the petition. Sentenced to 21 years' penal transportation, in 1856 Cuffay too received a pardon but chose to stay, working on as a tailor and becoming involved in local politics. He continued to organise and agitate for democratic rights in Tasmania until, living in poverty at the Hobart Invalid Depot, he died in 1870 at the age of 82.

As an interesting footnote to his life, it is worth mentioning that at an exhibition mounted in the UK Houses of Parliament in 2013, marking the 175th anniversary of the publication of the People's Charter, a copy of Byron's collected poetry was put on display that London Chartists had given to Cuffay, when he was transported, 'as a token of their sincere regard and affection for his genuine patriotism and moral worth'. [7]

∞

If any single Chartist could be said to have played the ultimate leading role in the movement as a whole, it was Feargus O'Connor. However after the 1848 fiasco of Kennington Common, the commanding six foot tall Irishman lost all credibility. It was bad enough that the petition contained a large number of forged signatures, but also held contemptible for falling so far short of the number he had touted. Laughed out of parliament when he took it upon himself to present the petition, it wasn't until July 1849 that the House of Commons belatedly carried out a vote, rejecting the People's Charter by 222 votes to 17.

Worse followed for O'Connor when his Land Plan was declared fraudulent and illegal in 1851. As the sole Chartist MP, he felt victimised in the House and took increasing exception to comments made by others when matters to do with Chartism were debated. This led on one occasion to him assaulting three other MPs and having to be arrested by the Deputy Sergeant-at-Arms before being excluded from proceedings. O'Connor's health was failing and he suffered a mental breakdown from which he did not recover.

By the end of 1851, weekly circulation figures of his vaunted Leeds-based Northern Star newspaper had slumped to 1,200 compared with the 50,000 in its 1839 heyday. In April 1852, he had sold the paper to the then editor George Julian Harney who merged it with the 'Friend of the People' to form the 'Star of Freedom'. The latter appeared in a smaller format to Northern Star and to avoid Stamp Duty printed no news. Even so, it was only to survive until December 1852.

Meanwhile in the spring of 1852, O'Connor went on a tour of America but returned amidst ever-increasing concerns over his health and well-being. The medical diagnosis eventually arrived at was that his apparent state of insanity was brought on by syphilis. O'Connor had never married but there had been a number of relationships. It was believed he had fathered several children over the years.

His sister made a decision to place him in Dr Thomas Harrington Tuke's private Manor House Asylum in Chiswick, where he remained until 1854. Then he was moved to his sister's house. He died on 30 August 1855, aged 59. On 10 September, he was buried in Kensal Green cemetery in London. It was estimated that 40,000 people took part in the funeral procession.

For a man who had given so much to the movement, most Chartists would have preferred to remember him for the undoubted qualities of character he had demonstrated as a strong leader in its formative years rather than for the evident shortcomings arising towards the end of his life.

∞

Many of the members who had served on the parliamentary select committee, taking evidence from McDouall in 1842, had been known for being radical in their outlook in comparison with the standards of their times.

Lord Ashley was to continue to try to improve the lives of workers by putting forward and supporting legislation which eased conditions in work-places. For example, he was a strong advocate of the Ten Hours Act, promoted by John Fielden, which was finally passed in Parliament in January 1847 and restricted the working hours of women and young persons between the ages of 13 and 18 to a maximum of ten hours a day.

To his credit, Lord Ashley was responsible in some way or other for the passage of nearly every labour bill from when he had first entered Parliament in 1826 onwards. In 1851, he was to take the title of 7th Earl of Shaftesbury upon the death of his father. However, he was to continue supporting the reform cause in the House of Lords up until his death in 1885, aged 74.

∞

Thomas Slingsby Duncombe, who was also a member of that 1842 select committee, had been MP for Hertford from 1826 to 1832 and then, more famously, MP for Finsbury from 1834 to 1861. Throughout his time in Parliament, he had been noted for his flamboyant manner and life-style. Talking of the Grant brothers being incorporated into his works by Dickens, the same author had parodied Duncombe's sartorial style of dressing in a brief sketch in Nicholas Nickleby.

Coming from a very wealthy family, he also had it going for him that he was generally recognised to be the handsomest and best dressed man in the house. His love for the theatre, women and gaming was well-publicised. His penchant for betting was though to land him in trouble, running up massive debts at the fashionable, exclusive gambling halls of the day, such as Crockfords and Almacks. To the tune of £120,000, estimated to be equivalent to £8 million in to-day's money. His creditors had him arrested in 1847 and he was criticised for using parliamentary privilege to escape punishment.

Between 1847 and 1850, due to a severe bronchial condition, Duncombe was too ill to attend Parliament regularly. However, when he did, he continued to stand up for the political rights of the less fortunate in society. Apart from taking on a campaign to secure the pardoning of Chartist John Frost, it was of course Duncombe who spoke up in the House in 1848 in favour of O'Connor's fateful petition.

With great affection, he was hailed by his Finsbury constituents as 'Honest Tom Duncombe'. To his detractors, he was known as the 'Dandy Demagogue'. He died in 1861 at the age of 65, buried in the same Kensal Green cemetery as O'Connor had been six years earlier.

∞

MPs Charles Villiers and Richard Cobden, also sitting on the 1842 select committee, were similarly radical in stance but much more in the direction of pursuing the cause of free trade. Villiers was elected as a Liberal MP for Wolverhampton in 1835. Before Cobden and Bright founded the Anti-Corn Law League, Villiers had been a lone voice in Parliament campaigning for the Repeal of the Corn Laws.

Eventually, he was to lay claim to two milestone achievements before his death in January 1898, aged 96. Firstly, as the oldest candidate, at the age of 93, to have won a parliamentary seat in an election. Secondly, as an MP from 1835 through to 1898, the distinction of being the longest continuous serving Member of Parliament in history.

Richard Cobden had, with John Bright, successfully fought for the Repeal of the Corn Law Act which finally came about in

1846. Subsequently, Cobden was instrumental in bringing about further free trade initiatives such as the Cobden-Chevalier Treaty of 1860, which established a strong trade connection with France. Suffering increasingly from bronchial problems, Cobden died on 2 April 1865 at the age of 60.

∞

Following his resignation as Prime Minister, worse personal tragedy was to ensue for Robert Peel when, on 29 June 1850, he was thrown from his horse while riding on Constitution Hill in London. The horse stumbled on top of him, and he died three days later on 2 July at the age of 62 as a result of a broken collarbone rupturing blood vessels.

His death was widely lamented and particularly so in the north-west of England. Son of namesake Sir Robert Peel, factory-owner and MP, the Peel family's connection with Bury and Ramsbottom struck a strong chord locally.

In the centre of Bury, a statue of Peel, sculpted by Sir Edward Hodges Baily (also famously known for his sculpture of Lord Nelson atop Nelson's Column in Trafalgar Square, London) was erected and opened to the public on Wednesday 8 September 1852.

In Ramsbottom, an even larger-scale project was carried out in the form of the huge 'Peel Monument', built on the brow of Holcombe Hill and designed to command the landscape for miles around. With £1,000 raised from public subscription, the scheme to bring this about had been the brainchild of remaining members of the Grant family, Daniel and John Grant. The Peel Monument, standing 1,100 feet (335 metres) above sea level, was officially opened the day after the inauguration of Baily's statue in Bury.

∞

Daniel Grant's health, which had taken a jolt following the death in 1842 of his brother William, had never seemed to pick up since then. Soon after, he had become embroiled in a long-running dispute with a railway company that was seeking to drive its Bury/ Rawtenstall line through the grounds of Springside. In the end, he settled for compensation at a rate which did not come cheaply for the company at £4,500, more than four times the amount raised for the Peel Monument.

Daniel died on 12 March 1855 from what was described on his death certificate as pulmonary and cerebral apoplexy. Compared with the grandiose tributes that had been paid to William though, Daniel's passing went relatively unnoticed beyond immediate family.

1855 was to prove a fairly brutal year as far as the remaining Grants, who had undertaken the journey down from Scotland back in 1783, were concerned. Less than two months after the death of Daniel, John, the last of the brothers, 'went to his rest'. Before the year closed, Jane, the widow of John Grant, also died. [8]

The Grant Estate thereafter passed into the hands of John and Jane's son, William. However, he possessed little of the appetite and few of the grafting qualities of the older generation Grants.

As mentioned earlier, the 1860s became much more difficult times for the cotton industry in Lancashire with the American Civil War playing havoc with supply of raw materials. In 1866, the Grants' business closed down and the Square works were taken over by Hepburn & Co. who used the premises for bleaching.

John Grant's Nuttall Hall was in 1928 to pass into the hands of local industrialist, Lt. Col. A.T. Porritt, who dedicated the surrounding land for community use in the form of various recreational facilities. The Hall itself was later to fall into disrepair and was demolished in 1952.

By way of a further footnote to the life of Daniel Grant, one more casualty of 1855 had been Elizabeth Brereton who died towards the end of that year, aged 55. Her death certificate cites epilepsy as the cause. It has been noted that 'medical ignorance at that time and the association of epilepsy with madness must have greatly affected sufferers. This would have added to the burden of the disease for her and for Daniel, and may well have been one of the reasons they never married'. [9]

Of their two children, the elder, Daniel Grant Brereton became an army officer and died in 1872 while the younger son Charles had passed away at the age of 21 in 1851 as a result of the epileptic condition inherited from his mother. He had not had chance to reap any benefit from the terms of the will his father had made out in 1847.

∞

Benjamin Disraeli, Conservative MP and novelist who had written the novel *Sybil: Two Nations* in 1845, managed very successfully to climb what he famously called the 'greasy pole of politics' to become Prime Minister.

The aftermath of events surrounding the Repeal of the Corn Laws in 1846 was to prove especially difficult for him. Out of his 44 years as an MP, he was to spend 33 of them in opposition. Throughout much of this time though, it remained Disraeli's belief that, if given the vote, British people would use it instinctively to put the Conservative Party into power. At a time of renewed agitation in 1867 for popular suffrage to be granted, in what was interpreted as a leap in the dark by many fellow-politicians, Disraeli persuaded a majority of the cabinet to agree to a new Reform Bill to supersede that of 1832.

Ultimately, the 1867 Reform Act was passed, which extended the franchise by 938,427 men – an increase of 88% on existing numbers. This was by no means deliverance of the universal suffrage put forward under the Charter but it did mark a considerable step forward.

Although Chartism had long since ceased to exist as a movement by this time, there must have been many former Chartists still alive who would have seen this development as amounting to something of a vindication of their efforts in the past.

As for Disraeli, his political career was to be a long, illustrious one. He died on 19 April 1881, aged 76.

∞

Bearing in mind the 'six points' of the Charter as a whole, what was to be the final outcome in terms of fulfilment of aims?

Although 1867 was to prove a significant leap forward, it would not be until the Representation of the People Act of 1918 that all men over the age of 21 and women over the age of 30 (following the successful impact of the Suffragette Movement) would be granted the vote. It was to take until 1928 before women of the age of 21 and over were included in the number.

In relation to the demand for secret balloting, Parliament would pass this in the Ballot Act of 1872. Meanwhile, the requirement for property qualifications for standing MPs had been ended in an Act of 1858. The demand for payment for MPs would have to wait though until the passing of an Act of Parliament of 1911. The Redistribution of Seats Act of 1885 was to address the expressed need for constituencies of equal size. In conclusion, the only one of the 'six points' that has failed to come about is that of 'annual parliaments' which has been continuously ruled out as making for a logistical nightmare.

Put in such a way, victory in the end was achieved for the cause of democracy. Even if Chartism was no longer in existence by the time any of the five measures above came to be enacted by Parliament, it could be argued that leaders of the movement such as McDouall had played vital roles in carrying out much of the preparatory groundwork.

In addition to this, the argument can be strongly put forward that 'most of the working-class movements that developed in the 1840s, '50s and '60s, in particular Co-operation and the miners' trade union, owed much to men who later had the satisfaction of witnessing the widespread acceptance of the programme for which they had fought'. [10]

∞

Given opportunity, how would McDouall have looked back on what was eventually accomplished? It may have provided certain consolation to him that progress was made in the end. Regrettably though, having a mindset impatient for immediate outcomes, irrespective of what materialised later, it is thought he would still have remained bitterly disappointed as a result of what little had been achieved in his own lifetime.

With 'ardent and fiery temperament', he had taken it upon himself to challenge and stoke up political upheaval in Britain on the same basis that revolutions, in the name of freedom and liberty, had successfully been engineered in America and France in the late 18th century.

McDouall was much more revolutionary than evolutionary in outlook. If he believed in a cause, he was not prepared to be baulked down the line. Even if he had remained alive to see the way in which improvements were gradually to come into effect, he would still have been contemptuous about the length of time the process took.

∞

It is important to bear in mind just how young McDouall was when he arrived in Ramsbottom in 1835 to start up his medical practice. He was still only in his early 20s when events took the dramatic turn they did for him at the start of 1839, catapulting him almost overnight into prominence as a Chartist leader with national status.

In the highly-charged and volatile atmosphere prevalent at the time, it was perhaps only understandable that the inexperienced newly-appointed young delegate, acting on the mood of his Ashton constituents, went off to London breathing fire and brimstone. McDouall's commitment to the tactic of using physical force to achieve Chartist objectives became almost non-negotiable from that point onwards. Other Chartist leaders counselled a more cautious response but it only drew his brash contempt. Instinctively, he felt that those holding office were never going to relinquish their tight control over the political system without a fight.

Both in terms of radical upbringing and his own temperament, McDouall showed he was never afraid to pit himself against authority if he felt the moral imperative to do so. The need to address the plight of workers, trapped inside the iniquitous factory system, was an issue he would never back away from. Nor the question of their right to vote in general elections.

Even if he knew to expect nothing less than relentless opposition from the authorities, McDouall found it equally difficult to contend with other Chartist leaders who saw the way to achieving success differently to himself. Always keen to strike while the iron was hot, he was endlessly frustrated by all the inherent delays built into time-consuming processes such as presenting petitions. He probably wouldn't have minded so much if they came to anything but the sad truth was they didn't. Apart from anything else, the endless dithering, as McDouall saw it, added to the personal pressures and sheer precariousness of scraping together a day-to-day living for delegates like himself. Without the necessary financial back-up, resources were stretched to breaking-point. Over time, he had found himself having to make far too many sacrifices, both in material and human terms.

In this sense, within a period of only a few years, he had 'exchanged the relatively comfortable existence of a doctor for a life of uncertainty and hardship in the "trade of agitation". Of course, all of this was 'at a time when the modern concept of professional politics had not won acceptance'. [11]

∞

Instead of accomplishing the tasks he had set himself at the start of 1839, he was worn down by setbacks, including two separate prison sentences in addition to his spell of exile in France, before dying in Australia in 1854, aged only 40.

It had been during time spent inside Kirkdale that he came to accept in retrospect that his life had essentially been about making sacrifices but without achieving core goals. The greatest sacrifice he had made, he now realised, was in human terms with his inability to be with and tend for the welfare of his wife and children. This was the supreme irony, and indeed ultimate tragedy, for a man who had valiantly committed himself to improving the lives of hundreds of thousands of other people across the country.

∞

Combing through the ranks of Chartist leaders, there is no more striking example than McDouall of a leader who demonstrated the courage of his convictions through thick and thin. His determination to be a champion of the people remains unquestionable. As an orator and inspiring influence on those who attended meetings to hear him speak, he had few equals. If he was hot-headed behind the scenes and prone to differences with colleagues, it could be said in his defence that this was more often than not because he felt so passionately about the issues that mattered to him.

∞

This chapter started off by speculating whether, had he lived beyond the age of 40, he would have written his memoirs. On a parallel note, it remains strange to think that, despite many articles covering aspects of his life, no full biography of McDouall has been written to this point.

Hopefully, this work will be seen as not only filling the gap but also providing a fitting tribute to the contribution made by a brave and principled man, ahead of his time, who dedicated himself to fighting so strongly on behalf of the dual causes of human justice and equality.

Notes on Sources

1. William Aitken, *Remembrances and Struggles of a Working Man for Bread and Liberty* p.14 - published by Tameside Leisure Services: Libraries and Heritage (1996).
2. Ashton News: 2 October 1869
3. McDouall's Chartist and Republican Journal: 15 May 1841.
4. Final declaration in *The Communist Manifesto* of Karl Marx and Friedrich Engels (1848)
5. E.P.Thompson, *The Making of the English Working Class* p. 902 - published by Harmondsworth (1980).
6. Quoted from '100 Great Black Britons' website 7.
7. Morning Star: 15 July 2013.
8. Hume Elliot, *The Story of the Cheeryble Grants* p. 211.
9. Alan Hitch, *Daniel Grant, Famous or Infamous?* P. 13.
10. Chris Aspin, *Lancashire: The First Industrial Society* p. 154.
11. Owen R. Ashton and Paul A. Pickering, *Friends of the People*, p. 23.

Nigel has a life-long interest in history, having studied for a degree in the subject at Cambridge University. He started out his career as a History teacher in 1971 before becoming a Secondary School Head Teacher in 1988. Coming to the Rossendale area as Head of Haslingden High School between 1996 and 2003, his last UK Head's post was at Kearsley Academy in Bolton from 2010 to 2014.

'Retired', he has carried out interim work abroad in the meantime, serving as Principal in Dubai in 2016 and presenting a teacher training programme in schools in New Delhi during 2018.

Much of Nigel's writing to date has taken the form of novels, with four publications:

- *The Inspector and the Superhead* (2000)
- *Cut and Run* (2006)
- *In a League of His Own* (2011)
- *Speed is of the Essence* (2015)

In 2020, he wrote *Come on you Rams*, the story of Northern Premier League football club, Ramsbottom United.

Living in the town since the mid-1990s, Nigel realises he is still reckoned 'an outsider' but hopes this biographical work, on another local theme, might go some further way towards qualifying him for acceptance as a local resident.